On the Old Saw:
That May Be Right
    in Theory
But It Won't Work
    in Practice

Works in Continental Philosophy

General Editor / John R. Silber

Immanuel Kant
ON THE OLD SAW:
THAT MAY BE RIGHT
in THEORY
BUT IT WON'T WORK
in PRACTICE

Translated by E. B. Ashton

Introduction by George Miller

University of Pennsylvania Press / Philadelphia

German title: *Über den Gemeinspruch: Das mag in der Theorie richtig
sein.*

Library of Congress Catalog Card Number: 73-83291

ISBN: (cloth): 0-8122-7677-9
ISBN: (paper): 0-8122-1058-1

Manufactured in the United States of America

In Memoriam

Fred Wieck

our now silent collaborator,
one of the last of the civilized editors

Editor's Foreword

Few people are so ignorant that they will dispute the value of theory. Yet men commonly denounce proposals that apply theory in daily life. Many of the finest insights of science, medicine, agriculture, ethics, law, and politics have been summarily rejected with the ritualistic formula: "That may be right in theory, but it won't work in practice." Fully appreciative of the enervating and pernicious influence of this nostrum, Kant published in 1793 the most rigorous and sustained critique that it or any other cliché has ever received.

Kant's essay, addressed to a broad intellectual audience, is one of the most neglected though most important documents of the Enlightenment. It is here published in English as a separate volume for the first time. Its relevance today depends least on its contribution to Kantian studies, though in "Theory and Practice" Kant elaborates significantly on the role of happiness in ethics and provides his clearest discussion of moral feelings and the nature of ethical motivation. Its importance for today derives primarily from Kant's brilliant discussion of critical political issues that are of intense contemporary interest—the nature of political authority, the right of revolution, freedom of the pen, the authority to make war, and the preservation of peace. Although these issues, raised by Hobbes, Locke and Rousseau, were central to political discussion at the founding of our Republic, their relevance even now is undiminished.

Kant examines the cliché from two general aspects. First, he discusses the problems involved in applying any theory and the paradoxical fact that there are theoreticians who lack the judgment (mother wit, or common sense) to apply theory effectively. But Kant argues that we cannot reject theory in any field on the basis of inadequate application: the soundness of theory depends upon its applicability, and inapplicability is clear evidence of incomplete theory or poor judgment. Second, Kant shows in terms of specific highly controversial examples that ethical and political theories, when intelligently interpreted and applied, work also in practice.

In the discussion of political theory, Kant develops a highly plausible contract theory of government. Seeing the social contract not as an historical fact but as a rational statement of the necessary conditions of social organization, Kant argues for limitations on the authority of both the sovereign and the people. Though Kant questions the right of revolution, he recognizes that the people "have inalienable rights against the head of state." In this regard he argues: "The citizen must be free to inform the public of his views on whatever in the sovereign decrees appears to him as a wrong against the community, and he must be granted this freedom by the sovereign himself." *"Freedom of the pen,"* Kant continues, ". . . is the sole shield of popular rights, for to deny the people this freedom would not merely deprive them of every claim to justice in regard to the supreme commander; . . . it would also deprive the supreme commander, whose will commands the subjects as citizens only by representing the general will of the people, of any knowledge of matters which he himself would change if only he knew them. Hence, to limit this freedom would bring him into contradiction with himself."

Kant, as shown by this example, thus offers a strong rational case for liberalism that is untouched by the rhetoric of contemporary radical and conservative criticism.

In the discussion of international law, Kant presents the rational, moral demand for world federation. Kant recognizes man's fascination with war: "Nowhere does human nature appear less lovable than in the relations of whole nations to each other. No state's independence or possessions are even for a moment safe from the others. The will to subjugate another, or encroach upon what belongs to him, is always present." And he argues that the "only possible remedy is international law based on public statutes backed by power." Kant's hope for world peace does not rest on an optimistic view of human nature but on his belief that "the distress of ceaseless warfare must compel men to adopt a . . . *federation* under jointly agreed international law." Laws and institutions are, according to Kant, essential if ethical and political theory are to work in practice. The preservation of peace will depend upon placing the decision to make war in the hands of the people. Kant writes: "Impotence must finally accomplish what good will ought to have done but did not: the organization of every state's internal affairs so that the decisive voice on whether or not to wage war is not that of the head of state—whom the war costs actually nothing—but that of the people, who pay for it."

Throughout this essay Kant exhibits his remarkable rational clarity and principled optimism along with his determined empiricism and historical doubts. "I put my trust in theory. At the same time, I trust in the nature of things, and also take account of human nature which I cannot, or will not, consider so steeped in evil that in the end reason should not triumph . . ." This is the hope or enlightenment of a practical man who knew that what is sound in theory must work in practice and that if "the crooked wood of human nature" is straightened by a rule of law, peace may yet prevail among men.

The introduction by Professor George Miller of the University of Cincinnati clearly defines the place of the essay in the philosophy of Kant and in the moral and political philosophy of his time. With Miller's full expository introduction, this should be a useful text in political science, history, and philosophy.

JOHN R. SILBER

Contents

* This translation is based on the German edition known as the *Akademie Aus-gabe: Kant's Gesammelte Schriften,* published by the Königlich Preussichen Akademie der Wissenschaften, Volume VIII, pages 273-313 (Berlin and Leip-zig, 1923. Walter de Gruyter & Co.). The approximate pagination of the Akademie Ausgabe is indicated at the foot of each page of the translation.

Introduction

"On the Old Saw: That may be right in theory but it won't work in practice" was published in 1793 in the *Berlinische Monatsschrift.*[1] Because of the issues it deals with, its style, and its place of publication, the essay is regarded as one of Kant's "popular works," as distinguished from his technical works on epistemology, ethics and aesthetics. This distinction may suggest that the popular essays are only of historical interest, dealing with problems unique to the 18th Century. But if one considers the issues discussed—freedom of the press, the need for world government, the limits of political obedience—the essays are as relevant as today's headlines. The distinction may also lead one to think that his technical works have little bearing on his views on popular issues, and that Kant's discussion of general issues sheds no light on his philosophical position. A reading of "On the Old Saw" should correct this misunderstanding, for here Kant attempts to show how his moral and political theories provide useful principles for effecting political reform. In addition, his discussion of issues like the "right to revolution" helps clarify features of his moral theory and his general approach to philosophical problems.

Kant here discusses the relationship between theory and practice from the standpoints, first, of a person faced with making moral decisions; next, of the statesman who must govern and the citizen concerned about the limits of political obedience; and finally of the individual who desires to know how he ought to act to realize a world government. And he attempts to show that the only course open to rational men is to act on the basis of Kant's moral and political principles that are valid both in theory and in practice.

THEORY AND PRACTICE

To understand Kant's conception of the relationship between theory and practice, we must clarify his views on the function of philosophy. Kant does not believe that philosophy is a purely theoretical activity whose aim is an intellectual comprehension of reality. While admitting that man is a rational animal who seeks to understand the world, the motivation to understand is, for Kant, rooted in the fact that man has to act. Unlike the other animals who simply respond to their natural desires and follow their natural inclinations, men are conscious of their impulses and aware of their conflicting and changing desires and inclination. This awareness causes a man to ask which inclination he ought to act upon or which desire to pursue, or whether to act on his inclinations or desires at all. Men have to decide how they are going to live their lives; they must make hard choices between alternative courses of action which they believe are open to them. On what basis are they to make these decisions? What sorts of principles or guides to action should they use? As Kant sees it, philosophy is directly relevant to the way in which a man conducts his life, particularly in those situations where the will plays a determining role.

Men want to know what principles they ought to use in making decisions. They are asking for a theory to guide their action. A theory, according to Kant, is a set of principles which specifies procedures to follow to achieve certain ends. It is, in a significant sense, a guide to action. Practice is the accomplishment of an end which, Kant claims, "is thought to follow certain generally conceived principles of procedure." [2] For Kant, practice is rational and purposeful action, involving an awareness of the end one wishes to achieve, and the realization that this end can be accomplished by means of some specified procedure.

One thing Kant attempts to show in all his writings is the role of theory in all distinctively human activities. To him, the role of theory is not only crucial in understanding moral and political behavior; it is also indispensable if we are to give an adequate account of our attempts to understand the world.

The natural sciences are those disciplines which provide insight into nature. The success of science is due largely to reliance on the experimental method, which involves the careful observation of nature. While Kant agrees that we must observe nature to gain understanding, observation alone, he insists, is not sufficient to gain understanding. For Kant, the significant discovery made by the proponents of the experimental method is not that we must observe nature to discover its laws; it is that observation is blind unless guided by theory. Accidental or random observations of nature never yield insight. Scientific observation is controlled and selective: it proceeds by means of carefully thought-out experiments designed in conformity with the principles of a theory. Theory tells one what to look for, and experiments are designed to yield observations which confirm a theory or require its modification or rejection. The relationship of the scientist to the natural order is not that of a "pupil who listens to everything that the teacher chooses to say", but that of a "judge who compels the witnesses to answer questions which he has himself formulated." [3]

Although for Kant a crucial test of any theory is its capacity to guide action in fruitful ways, and, accordingly, any theory is, in an important sense, grounded in experience, it would be wrong to assume that Kant believed the basic principles underlying the scientific investigation of nature to be generalizations from experience. Kant agreed with the empiricists that experience is the proper starting point for the construction of meaningful theories. But he opposed their assumption that if you start from experience, you must interpret the principles by which we render experience intelligible as empirical generalizations which future experience may falsify. Kant has two reasons for rejecting this conception of the basic principles of explanation; first, that it fails to accord with the status we ascribe to them; second, that if we conceive the basic principles as generalizations which may be false, we question the reliability of both our scientific and our ordinary knowledge of the world, and the possibility of any investigation of nature. The sciences, Kant believed, do provide knowledge of the natural order, and he was convinced that there is something wrong with any philosophical position which denies this. To him, one important task of philosophy is to elucidate and justify those principles used by scientists and ordinary men to understand the world.

The belief that the principles we use to organize our experience are empirical generalizations rests, Kant believed, on the assumption that the real is identical with the observable, that the observable is identical with the phenomenal given, and that the phenomenal given is or reduces to the content of sense perception. These assumptions underlie an empiricism which explains knowledge, moral experience, and other forms of human behavior in terms of the phenomenal given.

In the *Critique of Pure Reason,* Kant attempts to show the failure of empiricism to explain human knowledge. While the empiricist admits that we use certain principles to organize our experience, he holds that they are principles which future experience may falsify. He assumes that we can render experience intelligible without the use of these principles. Kant attempts to show that what the empiricist conceives as empirical generalizations are necessary conditions for the possibility of any kind of experience which we can render intelligible to ourselves. If Kant is correct, these principles cannot be falsified by future experience, for they must be presupposed as the conditions for having that experience. If we are to explain human knowledge, whether the kind with which science provides us or the basic perceptual knowledge which we all have of the world, then Kant insists we must grant the necessity of principles which cannot be understood as empirical generalizations.

Kant also claims that in scientific investigation and in our moral thinking we use certain high order theoretical notions which guide and direct our action. He uses the word "Ideas" for these notions, a word borrowed from Plato.[4] Like Plato's, Kant's Ideas are notions for which experience cannot provide an instance. But unlike Plato, Kant ascribes no metaphysical reality to Ideas. He interprets them as conceptions of goals which direct action in systematic ways. The conception of nature as the product of design is an Idea. Although it is not something we can know, either through experience or by logical demonstration, it is conducive to scientific investigation to think of nature in this way, for it is to conceive the natural order as an intelligible system. It stimulates the scientist to seek out order, which leads to the discovery of hitherto unknown connections statable in mechanical terms.

Ideas play an important role in our moral thinking, but not in stimulating us to discover connections in the world. We possess, Kant claims, conceptions of moral goals which ought to be actualized. As such, they are ends which men are obliged to realize through their efforts. Just as knowledge is an achievement dependent on the labor of scientists, so the realization of moral goals depends on what men do. For example, Kant claims that we are obliged to create a just civil state, and, he maintains, we have an idea of the characteristics of this state which tell us what we must do to realize it. But, Kant insists, whether the Idea is actualized depends not on the power of the Idea but on the action of individual men.[5]

Although Kant insists on the importance of theory in decision making, theory, he is aware, is not enough. One cannot become a successful scientist by mastering the proper principles for investigating nature, nor a skillful statesman by having at one's command sound political rules. Judgment is also required, which, for Kant, is the ability to determine "whether something . . . stand[s] under a given rule." [6] While theory can be taught, judgment is a "'natural gift," [7] a peculiar talent which can be practiced only.[8] Since there are no rules to guide or direct judgment, no theory can be developed to the point where decision making becomes a mechanical affair. While a theory provides principles which instruct us how to act in a given situation, there are no rules which tell us that a situation is an instance of a rule. Determining this requires judgment, and since judgment is an ability which all men do not have, progress in science and the realization of certain ideals depends as much on men of sound judgment as on sound theories.[9]

THEORY AND PRACTICE IN ETHICS

Just as Kant's epistemological views are clarified by contrasting them with those of the empiricist, so is his moral theory. He believed that the empiricist bias as to what experience reveals makes it impossible for the empiricist to account adequately for our moral experience, and, accordingly, leads him to construct a false moral theory. The empiricist holds that to understand morality, we must begin with what experience tells us about human nature and the values men seek. If we are to construct a moral theory that is a reliable guide to action, then, the empiricist insists, it must be consistent with these facts.

According to the empiricist, what makes an action morally praiseworthy is that it promotes some value which men seek. Experience, he maintains, reveals that happiness is what all men consciously seek, and that men understand the relationship between happiness and those means most conducive to its achievement. Since the task of ethics is to determine what men ought to do, this determination is an empirical enterprise. The job of the moral philosopher is to tell men what they ought to do, which is to inform them of those actions causally instrumental in attaining happiness. Ethics reduces to a set of rules which prescribe those actions most likely to promote human happiness.

Although, for Kant, we must turn to experience to discover both what men desire and those actions most conducive to achieving it, experience, he insists, shows us not how men ought to act, but only how they ought to act if they want to achieve certain ends. While what the empiricist tells us is interesting, Kant insists that it has nothing to do with morality. Kant maintains that they have overlooked crucial features of our moral experience. One feature is what Kant calls the "fact of moral obligation." Everyone, he insists, recognizes the clear difference between doing something because one wants to do it and doing it because he recognizes that he ought to do it. The experienced conflict between the two is just as much a fact about men as is the desire for happiness—and, Kant claims, it is a fact which the empiricist fails to explain. In addition, Kant insists that everyone acknowledges that the only actions deserving moral praise are those one performs because he recognizes that he ought to do them. That a person has performed what is considered a right action is not sufficient for saying that he acted morally. Something more is required, namely that he had the right reason for doing what he did. Kant claims that common sense reflection, when uncorrupted by the dialectics of philosophers, informs us that the feeling of moral obligation is distinct from the desire for happiness, and that the moral worth of a person's action is measured by his intention to do what he ought to do, and not by the supposed consequences of that action.[10]

The common man, Kant believed, knows what is right and what is wrong; he does not need the philosopher to tell him what he ought to do. Rather than providing us with moral rules, the moral philosopher is to explicate the principle or principles we use to determine how we ought to act, and to defend them against those who claim that morality reduces to a conflict between desires.[11] In addition, the moral philosopher must show that there are no sound arguments against the conditions for moral action. Given the relationship Kant believes holds between our common moral thinking, and the principles of his moral theory, it is hardly surprising that he is anxious to counter the charge that his theory will not work in practice.

In Part I of the essay Kant replies to the claim that there is a conflict between what his moral theory demands and what we can do in practice. The claim rests on three objections raised by Christian Garve.[12] Although attention will be restricted to the objections, these are not the only features of Part I worthy of attention.[13]

The first objection [14] is that Kant's moral theory requires, as a condition for acting morally, that one renounce the desire for happiness. Since we naturally seek happiness, his theory requires one to act contrary to his nature.[15] This persistent objection [16] rests on a basic misunderstanding of Kant's theory. Kant's theory does not require one to renounce the desire for happiness. Kant replies that one "cannot do so, nor can any other finite rational being." [17] What is required is that we not make the desire for happiness *the* or *a* condition for acting morally. In deciding what I ought to do, it is not a relevant consideration. But this is not to say that one must renounce it.

The second objection is to Kant's claim that I ought to do my duty simply because I recognize it as my duty. For Garve, it is "incomprehensible . . . how any man can be conscious of having achieved complete detachment from his desire for happiness, and thus having performed his duty quite unselfishly." [18] If, he reasons, I cannot know that I have acted for no other reason than that I recognized it as my duty, it makes no sense to say that I ought to act in this way. Nothing, Kant replies, follows from Garve's claim. Kant not only admits that "no man can ever be conscious with certainty of having performed his duty quite unselfishly" [19] but that it may be that no one either has or will do his duty. But, Kant observes, this does not show that I cannot do what is required of me. I may have done my duty for no other reason than that I recognized it as my duty, even though I am not certain of this. My being uncertain as to whether something was the reason for my action is consistent with the fact that it was. As long as it is not impossible for me to do what is required, I can do what I am obliged to do.

The third objection [20] is that in actual practice we are never sure which motive, duty, the desire for happiness, or some other motive or combination of them, actually carried the most weight in determining our action. Duty, it seems, is no clearer guide to action than any other motive, and, for the common man, plays no more important role in his decision making than do other conisderations. Hence, even though Kant's theory is a guide to action, it is no better than some other theory.

Apart from the insistence that his theory alone is consistent with acting morally, Kant argues that his theory, unlike that which makes happiness the ground of action, provides a reliable guide to action. While his theory informs one immediately of what ought to be done, this, Kant insists, is not true of the opposing one. To decide which action will promote my happiness "always requires a great deal of skill and thought." "The will thus pursuant to the maxim of happiness," Kant observes, "vacillates between motivations, wondering what it should resolve upon. For it considers the outcome, and that is most uncertain." [21] But, Kant claims, if one asks "where his duty lies, . . . he is instantly certain what he must do." [22]

THEORY AND PRACTICE IN CONSTITUTIONAL LAW

Two questions which have been asked as long as men have lived in civil society are (1) Why is a person obliged to obey the existing government? and (2) Under what circumstances, if any, is one justified in disobeying or in overthrowing the government? These questions were asked in Kant's lifetime, which was marked by the French and American Revolutions, and they are still being raised today. While it is acknowledged that existing governments can force a person to obey, one can ask whether the obligation to obey reduces to the recognition of superior force. Most of us believe that the obligation rests on more than the recognition of the power of governments. Submitting to superior force may be prudent; it is certainly not an obligation. What confers upon governments the authority which most of us believe they have? And under what conditions, if any, can a government lose its authority? Kant deals with these questions in Part II.[23]

In answering these above questions, Kant evaluates two influential theories which also provide answers. Each of the rival theories rests upon a conception of human nature, and each provides advice for governing the state. Although Kant rejects both theories, he does not reject everything included in them. In an important sense, his theory is a combination of what he considers the legitimate insights of the two. To understand Kant's theory, we must briefly characterize each theory and consider Kant's objections to them. The test Kant uses in evaluating the two is whether they are consistent with the conditions necessary for a stable society and whether they explain why men recognize that they are obliged to obey the government. The theories which Kant evaluates are versions of the Hobbesian and the Lockian theories.

HOBBESIAN THEORY

The Hobbesian explains the origin of civil society and the authority of government in terms of the conception of man as egoistic and anti-social. He explains why men move from the state of nature (a pre-societal condition) into civil society by identifying what causes them to do so. In the state of nature, men are essentially equal; there are no important differences between them. Whatever advantages in strength, intelligence or cunning one has over others is cancelled by advantages others have over him. In addition, since men are selfish and anti-social, they are indifferent to the concerns and interests of others. But to pursue his interests, one must have the power to prevent others from harming him. The consequence of these facts is that misery supremely characterizes the state of nature. Life for everyone is solitary, poor, nasty, brutish and short.

Men move into civil society because reason tells them that peace and tranquility are necessary for pursuing their own interests, and experience shows that this is impossible in the state of nature. It is in the self-interest of men to enter society, and since they are anti-social, this can be accomplished only by submitting to a power capable of ending the state of war. Whenever power is effective, men see the advantage in submitting to it, and the fact that one submits to superior power is interpreted as consent to it. What creates the obligation to obey is submission to the power of government, and what confers upon government its authority is the power to coerce. If a government loses its power, it thereby loses its authority.

For the Hobbesian there can be no circumstances under which one may disobey the government. Any laws which limit the obedience of the subject are never in the true interests of men. Since the absolute power of government is the condition necessary for civil society, there can be no right to disobey or to overthrow the government. There are two reasons men lack these rights. The first is that disobedience is irrational, for if the government falls, men return immediately to the state of nature or that condition which poses the greatest threat to their interests. Disobedience can never make things better; it can only make things worse. The second reason is that men have no rights. They move into civil society not to protect their rights but to end violence and strife. For this, one gives up his liberty, which, for the Hobbesian, is more a curse than a blessing. The only privileges which men have are those extended by government, and they enjoy them only so long as governments permit.

Kant agrees with the Hobbesian that a condition necessary for civil society is the power of government to coerce individuals, and that there is no right to disobey or overthrow existing governments. And while Kant insists that, at best, we only have hypotheses as to how and why men formed societies, the one he considers most plausible is similar to that advanced by the Hobbesian.[24] As Kant puts it, "universal violence and the resulting distress were finally bound to make a people decide that they would submit to the coercion of public laws . . . and found a state under a civil constitution."[25]

Despite the points of agreement, Kant opposes the Hobbesian theory. Kant rejects its basic assumption that an historical account of why and how men moved into civil society prescribes what the relationship between men and government ought to be. That one had good reasons for submitting to a superior power does not, in itself, establish that one is obliged to obey that power. For Kant, there is an important distinction between a government having the power to coerce and the right to coerce. While he agrees that having the power is necessary for a viable government, he disagrees that it thereby confers upon a government its authority. To claim that it does is to hold that might makes right.

Since Kant believes that every political theory is a guide to action, what advice does it give? It tells statesman and citizen alike that the only thing which men respect is power, and the question whether a government has the right to coerce is whether it has the power to do so. But, Kant observes, "once we are talking not of right but of power only, the people may try their own power and jeopardize every legal constitution."[26] If might makes right, the only way in which the citizen can determine whether he is obliged to obey is to test the power of government. The theory offers an open invitation to civil disobedience and revolutionary activity. To adopt the theory is to advocate policies the consequences of which would jeopardize or destroy the civil state.

The Hobbesian fails to see that men are more than egoistic and anti-social creatures who forfeit their liberty for the protection of government. They recognize that they have rights, and they are well aware of the difference between the power and the right to coerce. The theory fails to accord with the conditions necessary for a stable civil society and is also unable to explain why men recognize that they are obliged to obey the government.

THE LOCKIAN THEORY

The Lockian conceives of men as both reasonable and as constrained in their relationships with each other by considerations of morality. While each person pursues his own interests, most of us tend to respect the rights and interests of others. The Lockian therefore does not characterize the state of nature as a condition which drives men into civil society. Why, then, did they make the move? Men form civil societies because they find that the enjoyment of their rights in the state of nature is not as satisfactory as it could be. They find that their rights are sometimes threatened by those who are not constrained by moral considerations. While each man has a right to punish those who interfere with his rights, this is not always possible.[27] A related problem is that punishment by the victim may be inequitable, for in the state of nature, the victim is both the judge and the one who administers punishment. Civil society is created to deal with these problems.

The social contract is the instrument by means of which civil society is created. Via the contract, each individual gives up or transfers some of his natural rights (e.g., the right to punish) in exchange for the collective action and protection of a group. On this model, there are two agreements, one by which society is formed, and a second establishing an agency authorized to make and enforce laws.

The proper explanation of the origin of government is not the needs of men but their freely given consent. A man is obliged to obey the government because he has freely assumed that obligation. Whatever authority government has is that which the people give it. While there is an agreement between governed and government, it is more like that between the owner of a business and one who manages it than between equal parties. Since the function of government is to protect the rights of men, government may use its power only to this end. When it protects rights, it is justified in using force, and the obligation to obey is direct and complete. But when government uses its power in ways which do not serve the ends for which it was created or when it threatens the rights of men, it loses its authority. When government exceeds its authority, it harms the people, and the trust is broken. The people then have the right to disobey, to resist, and, if necessary, to overthrow the government. These rights derive from the natural right to protect oneself and to punish those who harm us.

Kant agrees that each individual "has inalienable rights which he cannot give up," [28] that each person "is himself entitled to judge" [29] these rights, and that it is the function of government to protect them. He also agrees that the idea of an original contract is the fundament "on which alone a civil and thus consistently legal constitution among men can be based and a community established." [30] One expects Kant to agree that men have a right to rebel against government if it fails to protect or transgresses these rights. But Kant does not take this step. To understand why we must get clear his interpretation of the relationship between the rights of the individual and the government, which is best understood in terms of his criticisms of the Lockian theory.

According to Kant, the Lockian fails to establish that a government has authority, even one which protects human rights, unless it is shown that it originated via some sort of contract, pact or agreement. The origins of most states are obscure, and what an historical investigation would probably reveal is that most, if not all, originated by means other than contract or agreement. Hence, to treat the social contract as an historical fact is dangerous, as it encourages disobedience or rebellion against existing governments.[31]

Even if we could show that a civil state originated via the consent of a group of individuals, how would this oblige the members of any now existing society to obey the government? While I can bind myself by an agreement, I cannot bind anyone who was not party to it. Kant holds that the Lockian theory is inconsistent with the conditions for a stable civil society and is unable to explain why we recognize that we are obliged to obey the government.

THE KANTIAN THEORY

For Kant, the importance of the idea of the social contract [32] is not that it explains the origin of the civil state; rather, it prescribes what the relationship between the individual and the state ought to be. It does not describe an event which took place in a remote "Golden Age" from which existing states have fallen; it is an ideal towards which states are obliged to move. The important points about the social contract are: (1) the insistence that the only rational justification for a civil state is the consent of the governed, and (2) the only morally justifiable use of government power is that to which all rational beings could agree. The social contract is both a norm we use to evaluate existing governments, and a program for reform. It is an "Idea of Reason," or a goal or end which we are obliged to actualize.

As Kant sees it, the purpose of a political theory is to explicate the conditions under which human rights are to be realized and the freedom of the individual secured. Kant asks: What form of civil society would rational beings create or how would they agree to be governed? They would, Kant answers, create a society *"allowing the greatest possible human freedom* in accordance with laws by which *the freedom of each is made to be consistent with that of all* others." [33] It would be a society in which the freedom of each individual extends only so far as it is compatible with that of every other individual. It would be a just society, guaranteeing and protecting the freedom of every individual. To accomplish this requires a system of positive public law, and a government with sufficient power to assure that the law is respected.

Kant agrees with the Lockian that the purpose of civil society is to serve the needs and ends of men, but, unlike the Lockian, he insists that these needs and ends can be provided for only in a civil society.[34] Kant also agrees that the function of government is to secure and protect human rights, but he claims that they can be secured only in a civil state. Unlike the Lockian, Kant claims that we are morally obliged to create and maintain civil society for this is the only way in which men can have rights and social justice can be achieved. For Kant, a right is not worth having unless it can be guaranteed, and guaranteeing it requires some means of informing others of what a person's rights are and of preventing others from infringing upon them. For example, in the state of nature, the right to freedom is the legitimate but unguaranteed claim to be left alone to pursue one's interests, as long as one does not infringe upon the freedom of others. Civil society guarantees this right, and, Kant claims, thereby gives one real freedom. He says,[35]

> We cannot say that men within a state have sacrificed a part of their inborn freedom for a specific purpose; they have in fact completely abandoned their wild and lawless freedom, in order to find again their entire and undiminished freedom in a state of lawful dependence.

Civil society also provides a greater guarantee that one will not unintentionally harm another. Outside of civil society, each person must decide what his rights are and determine when and to what extent another has infringed upon them. Since there is no government to appeal to for protection and justice, one must act against anyone he believes has harmed him. If someone has infringed upon my rights, he has harmed me, and justice demands that he be stopped and punished. But since the harmed individual must judge his own case and administer punishment, there is no assurance that the alleged offender has been treated fairly.[36] Men as we know them are not fully rational. They are creatures of limited knowledge and self-restraint, and, Kant recognizes, these limitations affect them when they judge and punish.[37] It is wrong to punish an innocent man, even in the sincere belief that he is guilty, and, Kant claims, we are obliged to eliminate situations in which this is likely to occur. Since the state of nature is such a situation, we are morally obliged to move away from it.[38] We ought to create a situation in which the rights of each person are made explicit through public laws, one in which there are public and clearly defined procedures and an impartial agency for determining whether one has been harmed, and an agency to punish those found guilty of harming others. While there can be no guarantee that this will prevent an innocent man from being harmed, it is a vast improvement over the state of nature.

For Kant, neither freedom nor the enjoyment of rights which flow from freedom are possible without law and government. The obligation to obey the government is prescribed by reason as necessary to secure human rights. Since we are morally obliged to treat every human being as an end and never as a means only, we are obliged to treat others as beings who have rights that ought to be protected. Hence, we are obliged to maintain the conditions under which rights can be protected. And since government and the rule of law are the conditions, we are obliged to obey the government and the law.

Although the ideal form of civil society confers upon its governing agency the authority which obliges me to obey, am I required to obey a government which does not accord with the ideal? If reason obliges us to actualize the ideal, we ought to change every existing government so that it does. And, it would seem, if, because of the resistance of a government, this is not possible, we are obliged to replace it with one that does. It seems that Kant's "Idea of Reason" is a call to action, and, given his sympathy for the ideals of the American and French Revolutions, a call for revolutionary action.[39] But if Kant claims that we must reject the Lockian and Hobbesian theories because they provide principles which, if acted upon, jeopardize existing states, is not Kant's theory subject to the same objection?

While we are obliged to reform existing governments, Kant denies that we have a right or obligation to replace them. We have an obligation and right to change every government by legal means, but there can be no justification for using illegal means to do so. Kant further claims that it is the lawmaker,[40] not the people, who is obliged to reform the government.[41] And just as the Idea of the social contract prescribes the ideal form of government, it also provides the lawmaker with the criterion which he ought to use in framing laws. The Idea obliges him "to frame . . . laws so that they might have come from the united will of an entire people." [42] The criterion is a test for determining whether a law is just. When framing a law, the lawmaker must ask whether *all* of the citizens could consent to it, even though there are circumstances in which some would not. If an entire people could not, under any circumstances, consent to it, it is an unjust law. But if it is possible that they all could, the law is just, and, Kant adds, everyone is obliged to obey a just law.

While we must obey a just law, and while the above test is a reasonable one for determining this, who administers the test? Contrary to the Lockian, Kant claims that the lawmaker and not the people decides whether a law is just. As far as the people are concerned, every law is just, and, accordingly, even though they are citizens of a state which does not accord with the ideal, they are obliged to obey.

Kant's point is not just that there must be an authority to decide whether a law is just, but that the authority must be consistent with the possibility of the rule of law. He believes that if the people, individually or collectively, were to make the final determination, this would be inconsistent with the rule of law. If each person were to decide, then a law would be both just and unjust, depending on the judgment of each person. And since one is not obliged to obey an unjust law, some would be obliged to obey while others would not. But a law is precisely the sort of thing which applies to everyone, and it applies to one regardless of what his beliefs about it may be. Hence, if the final determination were made by each person, the rule of law would be impossible. If the final determination were to be made by the people collectively, then either all of the people would have to agree, which, for the above reasons, is incompatible with the rule of law, or the people would have to establish a procedure or agency for making the final determination. While the latter is promising, it reduplicates the function assigned the lawmaker. For Kant, authorizing the lawmaker to decide is consistent with the rule of law.[43]

Although the people cannot decide whether a law is just, they have a right to question whether it is. Since one can at the same time question the justice of a law and acknowledge that he cannot make the final determination, questioning is consistent with the rule of law.[44] Rather than undermining the rule of law, Kant believed that allowing citizens to question the justice of law would strengthen the rule of law and would play a significant role in reforming the state. While the lawmaker alone is authorized to effect reform, Kant claims that he can embark on a wise policy of reform only if he is aware of the inequities in his laws and the shortcomings of his administration. For Kant, the Idea of the social contract obliges the lawmaker to recognize that citizen has a right "to inform the public of his views on whatever in the sovereign decrees appears to him as a wrong against the community."[45] An obedient subject must assume that any wrong done him by the government is unintentional, and that the lawmaker would change things if he were aware of the injustices. For Kant, to suppress the freedom of speech and the freedom of the press is to deprive the people of all hope of justice.

While a civil society based on the rule of law is the condition for securing human rights, what can the people do if the government fails to protect human rights or actually infringes upon them? Although the lawmaker is authorized to make laws, and the executive is authorized to enforce them, they are men and, accordingly, subject to the same limitations of rationality and self-restraint which make civil society necessary. Kant was aware of this problem. As he put it

> Man is an animal which, if it lives among others of its kind requires a master. For he certainly abuses his freedom with respect to other men, and although as a reasonable being he wishes to have a law which limits the freedom of all, his selfish animal impulses tempt him, where possible, to exempt himself from them. He thus requires a master, who will break his will and force him to obey a will that is universally valid, under which each can be free. But whence does he get this master? Only from the human race. But then the master is himself an animal, and needs a master. Let

> him begin it as he will, it is not to be seen how he can produce a magistracy which can maintain public justice and which is itself just, whether it be a single person or a group of several elected persons. For each of them will always abuse his freedom if he has none above him to exercise force in accord with the laws. The highest master should be just in himself, and yet a man. This task is therefore the hardest of all; indeed, its complete solution is impossible, for from such crooked wood as man is made of, nothing perfectly straight can be built.[46]

While government is necessary to protect my rights against the infringements of others, who will safeguard my rights against the greater threat of a tyrannical government?

While men have inalienable rights against the government, these rights cannot, Kant claims, "be coercive." [47] There is no legitimate way in which the government can be forced to respect human rights. Unlike the Lockian who considers the "right to revolution" a legitimate means of preventing governments from infringing upon rights, there is, for Kant, no such right. It is likely, he admits, that tyrannical governments will provoke their subjects to rebel, and he acknowledges that it is understandable why men resort to rebellion to secure their rights. And while Kant concedes that some revolutions make things better,[48] revolution, he insists, is never justified.[49]

If, Kant asks, there is a "right of revolution," then what kind of right is it? Is it a legal or a moral right? If it is a legal right, then it can be protected by law. And if it is a moral right, it must be the sort of thing which, if one claims it for himself, he must be willing to grant to another. Kant attempts to show that it is neither a legal nor moral right. And if it is some other kind of right, then, Kant argues, it is one which, if acted upon, threatens itself and all other rights.

If there is a legal right to revolution, it would have to be one which one could exercise only if it had been established that the government had harmed the people. This requires an agency whose function is to determine whether the government is in fact guilty of what it was charged. Hence, there would have to be an authority greater than the government, which, for Kant, means that the government would not be the government. In addition, if it had been established that the government was guilty, the government would be obliged to protect the individual when he exercises his right, i.e., when he is attempting to overthrow the government. These consequences rule out the possibility of a legal right of revolution.

Since there can be no legal way of determining whether a government has wronged the people, the "right to revolution" would have to be one which a person is justified in using when he believes that the government has harmed the people. It would presumably be a moral right. Kant's reply is that one may not claim a moral right to do something unless he is prepared as a rational man to extend that same right to another in a similar set of circumstances. But since one would not regard it as justified for another to overthrow the government just because he believed that the government had done wrong, one cannot claim such a right for oneself.[50] Without some procedure for establishing that a wrong has been done, the revolutionary, Kant insists, cannot know whether his action is justified. Kant is not demanding that we must be absolutely certain that a wrong was done, but that there be an objective way of deciding this.

Kant's major objection against the "right of revolution" is that it cannot qualify as a right because it is inconsistent with the conditions necessary for securing rights.[51] As we have seen, Kant insists that civil society with its rule of law is the only means of securing human rights. Hence, if one had a right to overthrow the government, one would be justified in engaging in an activity which, if universalized, would destroy every civil constitution and, as a consequence, negate the conditions under which one could have any rights at all.

Kant believes that his theory alone explicates the conditions for a stable civil society and explains why we recognize the obligation to obey the government. His theory provides the statesman with the principles for governing wisely and with a viable program for reform. Kant's advice to the statesman is that the way to maintain a stable society is to frame laws to which all of the citizens could consent, and to guarantee those rights, e.g., freedom of the press, which make it possible for them to play a significant role in re-forming the state. His theory tells the citizen that the only way in which his rights can be secured is in the civil state, which can be maintained only if the citizen recognizes his obligation to obey the law.

THEORY AND PRACTICE IN INTERNATIONAL LAW [52]

If the civil state shows that men can create the conditions for securing human rights, then, Kant asks, what do the relationships between nations tell us? There is no system of international law. The various nations are in a state of nature, for violence is the normal way in which nations settle their disputes. This condition ought to concern men, for the lawless and violent relationships between states pose a threat to the rights and freedom of men. Human rights can be guaranteed only in just civil states, and they can survive only in a world at peace under a system of international law.

Just as men are morally obliged to move into civil society, so nations are obliged to seek a relationship like that of the civil state. For Kant, this is the only way in which violence can be ended, and however impractical it may seem, it is an ideal which we are morally obliged to achieve. Cosmopolitan society is an Idea of Reason which sets a task for men. But unlike the Idea of the just civil state which provides principles for transforming what is into what ought to be, the Idea of cosmopolitan society demands that men create it. We are obliged to do this, and no appeal to experience or to the course of history can show it to be impossible. Indeed, we may assume that the realization of this goal may be helped by the course of history, for if it is plausible to assume that men were driven, against their natural inclinations, to create the civil state, so, Kant maintains, it is reasonable to assume that nations will also be driven to establish conditions under which a just system of international law can be established.

Although Kant holds that we are entitled to assume that there are historical tendencies which point in the direction of realizing the Idea, he reminds us that we can never have the kind of understanding of history which will assure us that this is inevitable. For just as history reveals tendencies in the direction of an international arrangement, so it also shows tendencies in the opposite direction. Lacking the assurance that cosmopolitan society is inevitable, it is important to see that the Idea is a task which reason demands men to achieve through their effort. And, Kant observes

> How great a gulf may still be left between an idea and its realization, are questions which no one can . . . answer. For the issue depends on freedom; and it is the power of freedom to pass beyond any and every specified limit.[53]

GEORGE MILLER

NOTES

1 "What is Enlightenment," "Idea for a Universal History from a Cosmopolitan Point of View," "Conjectural Beginning of Human History," and "The End of All Things" were published in this journal, which was one of the chief organs of the German Enlightenment. All of these essays are important for understanding Kant's overall position, and many are relevant to issues discussed in "On the Old Saw." All are included in *Kant on History*. Edited by L. W. Beck. New York: Library of Liberal Arts, 1963.

2 "On the Old Saw," p. 41.

3 I. Kant, *Critique of Pure Reason*. Translated by Norman Kemp Smith. New York: Macmillan & Co., 1958, Bxiii.

4 *Ibid.*, A313-B370.

5 The role Kant assigns to men in actualizing what ought to be anticipates Karl Marx. Both believe that ideals, regardless of their nobility, cannot alone alter or change things, insisting that transforming what is into what ought to be depends upon the action of men. The two differ in the interpretation of the role history plays in the actualization of what ought to be. Marx tends to find in history definite assurance that the action of men will be successful; Kant believes that while history reveals tendencies in the direction of what

ought to be, all that we can know is that the actualization of the ideal is not impossible. Thus, Kant places a greater emphasis on the importance of human action than does Marx.

6 Kant, *Critique of Pure Reason*, A133-B172.

7 "On the Old Saw," p. 41.

8 Kant, *Critique of Pure Reason*, A133-B172.

9 For an interesting account of the role of judgment in science, see Micheal Polanyi, *Personal Knowledge*. Chicago: The University of Chicago Press, 1958.

10 See Kant's "Groundwork of the Metaphysic of Morals." Translated by H. J. Paton in *The Moral Law*. London: Hutchinston University Library, 1964.

11 *Ibid.*, pp. 72-73.

12 Although Garve was a persistent critic, he and Kant were good friends. See Kant's letters to Garve, in *Kant's Philosophical Correspondence, 1759-99.* Translated and edited by Arnulf Zweig. Chicago: The University of Chicago Press, 1967, pp. 98-104 and 250ff.

13 Part I contains a nice discussion of Kant's understanding of the relationship between moral feelings and the motives of our action. See pp. 50-51. See also John Silber's "Introduction" to Kant's *Religion within the Limits of Reason Alone*. Translated by Theodore M. Greene and Hoyt H. Hudson. Harper Torchbooks, Harper and Brothers, New York: 1960, p. CX, n. 79.

14 "On the Old Saw," p. 46.

15 By implication there is the suggestion that the moral theory which is consistent with man's nature is that which makes the desire for happiness the ground of moral action.

16 See "Translator's Introduction" to Kant's *Foundations of the Metaphysic of Morals*. Translated by L. W. Beck. New York: Library of Liberal Arts, 1959, p. xviii. Beck cites it as a common criticism of Kant's ethics, which, Beck claims, is based on a basic misunderstanding of Kant's theory.

17 "On the Old Saw," pp. 45-46. See also John Silber's "Introduction," in Kant, *Religion within the Limits of Reason Alone*, pp. CXII-CXIII, n. 85.

18 "On the Old Saw," pp. 51-52.

19 *Ibid.*, p. 51. See also Kant, "Groundwork," in *The Moral Law*, pp. 74-75 and p. 87.

20 "On the Old Saw," p. 52ff.

21 *Ibid.*, p. 54

22 *Ibid.*, p. 54. See also Kant, "Groundwork," in *The Moral Law*, pp. 109-110.

23 This is not the only work in which Kant deals with these questions.

See Beck, *Kant on History;* Kant, *The Metaphysical Elements of Justice.* (Translated by John Ladd. Indianapolis: Library of Liberal Arts, 1965); and *Kant's Political Writings.* (Edited by Hans Reiss. Cambridge University Press, 1970).

24 For Kant's hypothesis as to how and why men moved into civil society, see his "Conjectural Beginning of Human History," in Beck, *Kant on History,* pp. 53-68.

25 "On the Old Saw," p. 78.

26 *Ibid.,* p. 74.

27 For an interesting discussion of the "natural right to punish," see J. G. Murphy, *Kant: The Philosophy of Right.* New York: Macmillan and Co., 1970, pp. 113-127.

28 "On the Old Saw," p. 72.

29 *Ibid.,* p. 72.

30 *Ibid.,* p. 65.

31 *Ibid.,* pp. 69-70. See also Kant's *The Metaphysical Elements of Justice,* and Reiss, *Kant's Political Writings,* p. 143.

32 Kant's conception of the social contract is more like Rousseau's than Locke's. See Ernst Cassirer's excellent essay, "Kant and Rousseau," *Rousseau, Kant and Goethe.* New York: Harper and Row, 1963, p. 25ff.

33 Kant, *Critique of Pure Reason,* A317-B373.

34 Kant also claims that "the development of all the capacities which can be achieved by mankind, is attainable only in society." See "Idea for a Universal History," in Beck, *Kant on History,* p. 16.

35 Kant, *The Metaphysical Elements of Justice,* p. 140.

36 *Ibid.,* p. 137.

37 For an extended discussion of this point, see Murphy, *Kant: The Philosophy of Right,* pp. 123-124.

38 Kant, *The Metaphysical Elements of Justice,* p. 137.

39 See L. W. Beck, "Kant and the Right of Revolution," *Journal of the History of Ideas.* XXXII, No. 3 (July-Sept. 1971), pp. 411-422; and H. S. Reiss, "Kant and the Right of Rebellion," *Journal of the History of Ideas.* XVII (1965), pp. 179-192. Although Kant never wavered in his support of the ideals of the French Revolution, he was very concerned about its violence. See Charles W. Hendel, "Freedom, Democracy and Peace," *The Philosophy of Kant and the Modern World.* Edited by C. W. Hendel. New York: The Library of Liberal Arts, 1957, p. 108-109.

40 Although I will use the term "lawmaker," it is correct to refer to the legislature or the law-making body. For an explicit account of the

structure of government, see Kant, *The Metaphysical Elements of Justice*, pp. 141-143.

41 Although the lawmaker has a right to reform the government, he has no right to transform it from, for example, an aristocracy into a democracy. See Beck, "Kant on the Right of Revolution," p. 416.

42 "On the Old Saw," p. 65. While the lawmaker is authorized to make the law, he is not authorized to enforce it. This is the task of the executive, who is subject to the law. Kant, *The Metaphysical Elements of Justice*, pp. 141-143.

43 A good analogy is the role of the Supreme Court of the United States in determining the constitutionality of a law. While Kant insists upon a government of laws and not of men, he realized that men must be assigned an important role if there is to be a rule of law.

44 See Kant, "What is Enlightenment," Beck, *Kant on History*, pp. 3-10.

45 "On the Old Saw," p. 72.

46 Kant, "Idea for a Universal History," in Beck, *Kant on History*, pp. 17-18.

47 "On the Old Saw," p. 71.

48 Kant, "Perpetual Peace," in Beck, *Kant on History*, p. 120, n. 1.

49 Although revolution is never justified, Kant holds that once a revolution has taken place, any attempt to undo it or to re-establish the old order is wrong. We have a duty to obey the new government, even though it originated illegally. Kant, *The Metaphysical Elements of Justice*, p. 147.

50 For a complete discussion of this argument, see Murphy, *Kant: The Philosophy of Right*, pp. 136-138. For an interesting discussion of the "right of resistance," which often takes forms different from the violent activity associated with revolution, see pp. 138-139.

51 It seems that passive disobedience is a form of resistance against the government which is not inconsistent with the rule of law, particularly when those who resort to it acknowledge that the government has a right to arrest and imprison them. For an interesting discussion of the justification of civil disobedience, see John Rawl's *A Theory of Justice*. Cambridge: Harvard University Press, 1971, p. 371ff.

52 For a more complete discussion of this issue, see Kant's "Perpetual Peace," in Beck, *Kant on History*, pp. 85-135. Appendix I to the essay, pp. 117-128, is particularly relevant.

53 Kant, *Critique of Pure Reason*, pp. A317-B374.

On the Old Saw:
That May Be Right
in Theory
But It Won't Work
in Practice

A set of rules, even practical rules, is called a *theory* if the rules are conceived as principles of a certain generality and are abstracted from a multitude of conditions which necessarily influence their application. Conversely, we do not give the name *practice* to every activity, only to that accomplishment of an end which is thought to follow certain generally conceived principles of procedure.

However complete the theory may be, it is obvious that between theory and practice there must be a link, a connection and transition from one to the other. To the intellectual concept that contains the rule, an act of judgment must be added whereby the practitioner distinguishes whether or not something is an instance of the rule. And since we cannot always lay down rules for our judgment to observe in subsumption (as this would go on ad infinitum), there may be theoreticians who, for lack of judgment, can never be practical: physicians or jurists, for example, who have been well schooled but do not know what to do when they are summoned to a consultation.

But even where we find this natural gift, there may be a lack of premises. The theory may be incomplete, perhaps to be supplemented only by additional experiments and experiences from which the trained physician, agriculturist, or economist can and should abstract new rules of his own, to complete his theory. Thus, when the theory did not work too well in practice, the fault lay, not in the theory, but rather in there being *not enough* theory which a man should have learned from experience; and which is true theory even though he cannot express it or, as a teacher, expound it systematically in general propositions, and thus he cannot claim to be a theoretical physician, agriculturist, etc.

Accordingly, no man claiming to be practically versed in a science can disdain its theory without exposing himself as an ignoramus in his field. It is the belief of such a man that he can get farther than theory might take him by fumbling with experiments and experiences without specific principles for organizing them (which properly constitutes what we call "theory") and without an overall conception of his business (which, when pursued methodically, is called a "system").

And yet, when an ignorant individual calls theory unnecessary and dispensable in his supposed practice, this is not as unbearable as when a know-it-all admits its academic value (as a mere mental exercise, perhaps) while asserting that in practice things look altogether different, that with one's emergence from school into the world comes an awareness of having pursued empty ideals and philosophical dreams—in a word, that what sounds good in theory is invalid in practice. (Which is often put this way: that some proposition or other does apply *in thesi*, but not *in hypothesi*.) Now, if an empirical machinist said of general mechanics, or an artilleryman of the mathematical doctrine of ballistics, that the theory is nicely thought out but not at all valid in practice because the experience of applying it yields very different results, one would simply laugh at them. For if the first were to consider the theory of friction, and the second that of air resistance—that is, if they were to add more theory—their theories would conform very well to experience. Still, matters are altogether different with a theory that concerns objects which can be observed, and with one concerning objects represented merely by concepts (such as the objects of mathematics and those of philosophy). Although from the standpoint of reason the latter objects may indeed and unimpeachably be *thought*, they are perhaps not *given* at all; they may be nothing but empty ideas that in practice are put either to no use at all or to a detrimental use. In such cases, therefore, that old saw might be perfectly appropriate.

In a theory based on the *concept of duty*, however, there need be no concern about empty ideality. For the pursuit of a certain effect of our will would be no duty if the effect were not also possible in experience (whether conceived as complete, or as constantly approaching completion); and this is the only kind of theory we are discussing in the present essay. About this theory the philosophically scandalous pretense is not infrequently advanced—that what may be true in it is still invalid in practice. And this pretense is advanced in a tone of lofty disdain full of presumption to have reason itself reformed by experience in the area which reason deems its highest honor, and with the sapient conceit to see farther and more clearly with the eyes of a mole, fixed upon experience, than with the eyes of a being that was made to stand erect and to behold the heavens.

This maxim, grown very common in our talkative, actionless times, does most harm when it refers to questions of ethics (to moral or legal duty). For these are matters of the canon of reasons (in the practical realm), where the value of practice depends entirely on its appropriateness to the underlying theory. All is lost if empirical and therefore accidental conditions of the application of the law are turned into conditions of the law itself, and thus a practice calculated for an outcome probable in line with *past* experience is made master of the self-existing theory.

I divide this essay according to the three standpoints from which a gentleman bold enough thus to pronounce on theories and systems usually judges his object. That is, in three qualities: 1. as a private person yet a *man of business,* 2. as a *statesman,* and 3. as a *man in the world* (or, a world citizen generally). These three persons are agreed to have at the *man of the academy,* who works on theory in their behalf and to their benefit; imagining that they know better, they mean to banish him to his academy (*illa se iactet in aula!*—Let him shine in the lecture hall!), as a pedant unfit for practice and a mere obstacle in the way of their experienced wisdom.

Accordingly, we shall present the relationship of theory and practice in three parts: first, in morality in general (with regard to the welfare of each *human being*); second, in politics (with respect to the welfare of *states*); third, in a cosmopolitan perspective (regarding the welfare of the *human race* as a whole and assuming that progress in that direction is made in the generational sequence of all times to come). For reasons apparent from the essay itself, the subtitles will express the relationship of theory and practice in *morality,* in *constitutional law,* and in *international law.*

I. On the Relation of Theory to Practice in Morality in General

(in reply to some exceptions taken by Professor Garve)*

Before I come to the real point at issue—namely, what in the use of one and the same concept may be valid only in theory or only in practice—I must compare my theory, as set forth elsewhere, with Herr Garve's notion of it, to see beforehand whether we understand each other.

A. Provisionally, by way of introduction, I had defined ethics as a science that teaches, not how we are to achieve happiness, but how we are to become worthy of happiness.** My definition, as I had not failed to note, does not mean that in matters of obeying duty a man should *renounce* his natural goal of happiness. He cannot do so,

---

* *Versuche über verschiedne Gegenstände aus der Moral und Literatur* (Essays on Several Subjects from the Realm of Ethics and Literature) by Ch. Garve, Part One, pp. 111-116. I call the denial of my theses "exceptions" taken by this worthy man to points on which (I hope) he wants to come to an understanding with me. I do not call them "attacks," derogatory statements designed to provoke a defense for which there is neither a place here nor an inclination on my part.

** Being worthy of happiness is a personal quality based on the subject's own will. Due to this quality, a generally legislative reason (one making laws for nature as well as for free will) would harmonize with all of a person's ends. Hence it is totally different from skill in the achievement of some kind of happiness. For a man is not worthy even of this skill, nor of the talent for it lent to him by nature, if his will does not conform to, and cannot be contained in, the only will fit for a universal legislation of reason (i.e., if it is a will that conflicts with morality).

nor can any other finite rational being. What I mean is that, when duty calls, he must completely *abstract* from this consideration. Under no circumstances must he turn it into a *condition* of obeying the law prescribed to him by reason; indeed, he must seek as best he can to be conscious that no *motive* derived from it has imperceptibly mingled with his definition of his duty, as will happen because we tend to conceive duty as linked with sacrifices exacted by its observance (by virtue) rather than with the benefits it confers. The point is to bring the call of duty to mind in its totality, as demanding unconditional obedience, as self-sufficient, and as requiring no other influence.

a. Herr Garve puts my thesis as follows: "Kant maintained that observance of the moral law quite irrespective of happiness is man's *sole ultimate end,* that it must be viewed as the sole end of the Creator." (According to my theory, the sole end of the Creator is neither the morality of man alone nor happiness alone; instead, it is the highest good possible in the world: the union and concordance of the two.)

B. I had further remarked that this concept of duty need not be based upon any particular end, but that, rather, it *introduced* another end for the human will: namely, to strive as best he can for the *highest good* that is possible in the world (universal happiness linked to and in accordance with the purest morality in the world as a whole). Since this is within our power on the one side, but not on both, its effect *as a practical end* is to constrain men of reason to believe in a moral world governor and in a life to come—not as if both had to be presumed in order to give the general concept of duty "support and firmness," i.e. a safe ground and the required strong *motivating force,* but only so that an *object* is provided for this ideal of pure reason.* For duty in itself is nothing

---

* The need to assume a *highest good* in the world made possible with our cooperation, as the ultimate end of all things is due, not to a lack of moral motivations. It is due rather to external conditions in which alone, and in accordance with the motivating forces, an object can be brought forth as an end in itself (as the moral *ultimate end*). For without an end there cannot be any

but the will's *restriction* to the condition of a universal legislation made possible by an accepted maxim—the object of the will, or the purpose may be anything whatever (hence even happiness) provided the object, or any purpose we may have, is completely abstracted from. When we ask about the *principle* of morals, the doctrine of the *highest good* as the ultimate end of a will that is in conformity to its laws, can thus be wholly ignored and put aside as episodic; and indeed we shall see later that where the real issue is at stake, no attention at all is paid to this doctrine, only to the universal moral standpoint.

b. Herr Garve covers these theses in the following expressions: "that a virtuous man can never, nor must he ever lose sight of this aspect (his own happiness), for otherwise he would utterly lose his

---

will—although, where legal compulsion of actions alone is involved, one must abstract from the end, and the law alone constitutes the ground that determines the will. Not every end is moral, however, (not, for example, that of one's own happiness); but the moral end must be unselfish. And the need for an ultimate end established by pure reason and comprising the entirety of all ends under one principle (a world as the highest good possible through our collaboration) is a need of the unselfish will that *expands,* beyond the observance of formal laws, to the production of an object (the highest good). This determination of the will is of a special sort, namely, determination by the idea of the entirety of all ends. Its basis is that *if* we stand in certain moral relationships to things in the world, we must obey the moral law in every respect; and there is, moreover, a duty to strive with all one's abilities so *that* such a relationship (a world in accordance with the highest moral ends) will exist. Man conceives himself here in analogy to the deity which, although subjectively requiring no outward thing, nevertheless cannot be conceived as secluded within itself, but only as destined to bring forth the highest good outside itself by the very sense of its own all-sufficiency. In the supreme being, this necessity (which in man is a duty) can not be conceived by us otherwise than as a moral need. In man, therefore, the motive force lies in the idea of the highest good possible through his efforts. The motivation is not the happiness he means to gain for himself in this cooperation; it is rather that idea as an end in itself and, hence, its pursuit as duty. For the idea contains not the prospect of happiness pure and simple, but only that of a proportion between happiness and the worthiness of whichever subject it may concern. When a will is determined, however, by limiting itself and its purpose to the restrictive condition of belonging to such an entirety, it is *not selfish.*

way to the invisible world, to a conviction of God's existence and of
immortality. But this conviction, according to that theory, is absolutely necessary *to give support and firmness to the moral system.*"
And he concludes with this crisp and pithy summary of the asser-
tions attributed to me: "A virtuous man, in accordance with those
principles, will strive incessantly to be worthy of happiness; but
insofar as he is truly virtuous, he will never strive to be happy."
(Here the word "insofar" causes an ambiguity that must first be
straightened out. It may mean that, being virtuous, one bows to his
duty *in the act;* in this sense the sentence fully accords with my
theory. Or it may mean that if one is really virtuous, or in other
words, that even if duty is not involved and there is no conflict with
it, the virtuous man ought never to consider happiness at all. In that
sense it is a flat contradiction of my statements.)

These exceptions are thus nothing but misunderstandings (for I
would not wish to consider them misinterpretations). The possibility
of their occurrence would be puzzling if the human tendency to
follow one's own habitual trains of thought even in the evaluation
of the thoughts of others, and thus to carry one's own thinking into
theirs, did not suffice to explain such a phenomenon.

This polemical treatment of the moral principle just cited is
followed then by a dogmatic statement to the contrary. Herr G.
comes to this analytical conclusion: "In the order of *concepts,* the
perceiving and distinguishing acts in which we *prefer* one condition
to another must precede our choice of either, and thus precede the
predetermination of a specific end. But if a creature endowed
with consciousness of itself and its condition *prefers* a present and
perceived condition to others, this condition is a *good* one; and a
series of such good conditions is the most general concept, ex-
pressed by the word *happiness.*" Moreover: "A law presupposes
motives, but motives presuppose a previously perceived difference
between a condition that is worse and one that is better. This perceived difference is the element of the concept of happiness," etc.
And further: "*From happiness,* in the most general sense of the
word, *spring the motives for every endeavor,* including that for
compliance with the moral law. I must know that something is good

before I can ask whether the fulfillment of my moral duties comes under the rubric of the good. Man must have a *motivational drive* that puts him in motion *before* a goal can be set for him,* indicating where the motion ought go."

This argument is nothing but a play on the ambiguity of the word "good." Either the good is absolutely good, good in itself as opposed to evil in itself, or it is never more than conditionally good, being compared with the good that is worse or better since the state chosen as better may be only a comparatively better state though in itself it is still evil.

The maxim that a categorically commanding law of the freely choosing will should be observed absolutely, regardless of underlying ends (that is, duty) differs essentially, i.e., *in kind,* from the maxim to pursue an end supplied by nature itself as our motive for some sort of action (the end generally called happiness). For the first is good in itself, while the second is far from it; in the event of a clash with duty, it may be very evil. On the other hand, if the basis is a certain end and there is thus no law that commands absolutely (if the law commands only under the conditions of that end), two opposite courses of action may both be conditionally good though one is better than the other (which would then be called comparatively evil). They do not differ *in kind, merely in degree.* And this is the case with all acts not motivated by the absolute law of reason (by duty), but by an end arbitrarily proposed by ourselves. For that end is part of the sum of all ends, whose attainment we call happiness; and one act can do more for my happiness, the other less, so that each can be better or worse than the other.

But *preferring* one state of determining the will to another is simply a free act (*res merae facultatis,* as the lawyers say). It is an act in which no consideration is given to the question whether the

---

* This, after all, is precisely what I am urging. The motivational drive which a person can have in advance, before a goal (an end) is set for him, can obviously be nothing other than the law itself, through the respect it instills (whatever ends one may have and may attain by compliance). For in regard to the formal element of choosing, the law is all that remains once the substance of choosing (the goal, as Herr G. calls it) is left out of consideration.

determination of will is good or evil in itself, and in which alternatives are therefore equivalent.

A state of being in line with a certain *given end* which I prefer to any other end *of its kind* is a comparatively better state in the field of happiness (which *reason* never acknowledges as other than conditionally *good* to the extent that one is worthy of it). But the state in which I consciously prefer to do my duty, when there is a conflict between certain of my ends and the moral law of duty, is not merely a better state; it is the only condition that is good in itself. It is a good from an altogether different field, a field in which ends that may suggest themselves to me (and their sum total, happiness) will not even be considered, and in which the determining ground of the choosing will is not its material (an object on which the choosing is based) but the mere form of the universal lawfulenss of its maxim.

By no means, therefore, can one say that every state I *prefer* tó any other kind is classified as happiness by me. I must first be sure that I am not acting counter to my duty; not until then am I permitted to look for all the happiness compatible with my morally (not physically) good state.*

True, the will must have *motives;* but these are not specific objects presumed as ends and relating to *physical feelings.* They are nothing but the unconditioned *law* itself, and the will's receptivity in subjecting itself to that law as an unconditional constraint is called *moral feelings.* This is not the cause but the effect of the will's determination, of which we would not have the slightest inner

---

* Happiness contains whatever (and no more than) nature can obtain for us; but virtue contains what nobody but a person himself can give to or take from himself. If one countered that by straying from the path of virtue a person can at least bring recrimination and pure moral self-reproach with accompanying discontent upon himself, and that, consequently, he can make himself unhappy, we may concede that much. Yet none but the virtuous, or he who is about to become virtuous, is capable of this pure moral discontent (not with the disadvantages resulting from his act, but with its sheer illegality). The discontent is thus not the cause but rather the effect of his being virtuous, and the ground that motivated him to be virtuous could not come from that unhappiness (if the pain following a misdeed be so called).

perception if that inner constraint were not already present within us. This is why the old litany—that this feeling (and thus a pleasure which we make our end) constitutes the will's first determining cause, and that happiness (of which that pleasure is an element) therefore constitutes the ground of all objective necessity to act, hence of all obligation—is just a toying with rationalizations. For if we are incapable of ceasing to ask questions when a cause has been proposed for a certain effect, we will in the end turn the effect into its own cause.

Now I come to the point that properly concerns us here: to exemplify and test the interests of theory and practice that presumably conflict in philosophy. Herr G., in the treatise cited above, provides the best example. First (speaking of the difference I note between a doctrine that teaches how to become *happy* and one that teaches how to become *worthy* of happiness) he says: "For my own part I confess that I fully comprehend this division of ideas in my *mind,* but that I cannot find this division of wishes and strivings in my *heart,* that in fact it is incomprehensible to me how any man can be conscious of having achieved complete detachment from his desire for happiness, and thus having performed his duty quite unselfishly."

I shall answer the latter point first. I gladly admit that no man can ever be conscious with certainty of *having performed* his duty quite unselfishly, for this is a matter of internal experience, and this consciousness of his state of mind would require one to have a consistently clear view of all the subsidiary notions and considerations which imagination, habit, and inclination attach to the concept of duty. We can never demand such a view, nor can the nonbeing of something (as of some hidden weighing of benefits) be an object of experience. But that man *ought to perform* his duty quite unselfishly, and that his desire for happiness *must* be completely divorced from his concept of duty in order to preserve its purity—this he knows with the utmost clarity. Or, should he believe that he does not, this can be required of him to the best of his ability. For it is precisely in that purity of the concept of duty that the true worth of morality is found, and thus one must be capable of it. Perhaps no person has ever been quite unselfish (without an admixture of other motives) in doing what he recognized and also revered as his duty; perhaps, despite the greatest striving, no one will ever get that far. But each person is able—and as far as the fulfillment of his duty is concerned, this suffices—to scrutinize himself painstakingly and to perceive not only an absence of any such participating motives, but also to become aware of self-denial in regard to many motives at odds with the idea of duty, or, consequently, with the maxim to strive toward this purity. On the other hand, to make a maxim of favoring the influence of such motives, on the pretext that human nature does not allow this kind of purity (which also cannot be stated with certainty), is the death of all morality.

As for Herr G.'s previously quoted confession of being unable to find that division (more properly, that detachment) in his *heart,* I do not hesitate to deny his self-accusation outright and to defend his heart against his mind. In his heart (in determining his will) this honest man has always found that kind of detachment. It was in his mind only, for purposes of speculation and of seeking to comprehend the incomprehensible (inexplicable)—to wit, the possibility of categorical imperatives (such as the imperatives of duty)—that the detachment would not fit in with accustomed principles of psychological explanation (all built upon the mechanism of natural necessity).*

But then Herr G. concludes: "Such niceties in the distinction of ideas grow *dim* when we merely reflect on particular objects; but

---

* In Prof. Garve's *Notes to Cicero's Book on Duties,* p. 69, 1783 edition, we find a remarkable admission worthy of his perspicacity: that freedom, according to his inmost conviction, would "always remain unfathomable and never be explained." There is simply no proof of its actuality to be found in direct or indirect experience—and without any proof one cannot simply assume it. Freedom is demonstrable, then, not on purely theoretical grounds (for these would have to be sought in experience), but by means of theses of purely practical reason—and not of technical-practical theses either (for those again would require empirical grounds), but of moral-practical ones only; so we cannot help wondering why Herr G. did not resort to the concept of freedom to save at least the possibility of such imperatives.

they *evaporate altogether* when it comes to action, when the ideas are to be applied to desires and intentions. The simpler, the quicker, *the less clearly conceived* our step from reflecting on motives to real action, the smaller our chance to know precisely and surely just how much weight each motive carried in guiding the step this way rather than another." And on this I must contradict him loudly and zealously.

The concept of duty in its total purity is not only incomparably simpler, clearer, and more comprehensible and natural for everyone's practical use than any motive drawn from happiness, or mixed with happiness and with considerations of happiness (which always require a great deal of skill and thought). In the view of even the most common human reason, the concept of duty is far stronger, more *penetrating*, and more promising than any motives borrowed from the self-interested principle of happiness—provided only it is presented to our will in detachment from, or even in opposition to, those considerations of happiness.

Suppose, for instance, that someone is holding another's property in trust (a deposit) whose owner is dead, and that the owner's heirs do not know and can never hear about it. Present this case even to a child of eight or nine, and add that, through no fault of his, the trustee's fortunes are at lowest ebb, that he sees a sad family around him, a wife and children disheartened by want. From all of this he would be instantly delivered by appropriating the deposit. And further that the man is kind and charitable, while those heirs are rich, loveless, extremely extravagant spendthrifts, so that this addition to their wealth might as well be thrown into the sea. And then ask whether under these circumstances it might be deemed permissible to convert the deposit to one's own use. Without doubt, anyone asked will answer "No!"—and in lieu of grounds he can merely say: "It is wrong!", i.e., it conflicts with duty. Nothing is clearer than that. And assuredly it is not his own *happiness* that the man promotes by surrendering the deposit. For if happiness were the end that he expected to determine his decision, he might, for example, think along these lines: "If you give up, unasked, what does not belong to you, you will gain a widespread good reputation that may become quite lucrative for you." But all this is very uncertain. On the other hand, many misgivings arise as well: "To end your straitened condition at one stroke, you might embezzle what has been entrusted to you; but if you made prompt use of it, you would evoke suspicions concerning how and by what means your circumstances had so quickly improved; however, if you were slow about it, your distress would increase in the meantime to a point beyond help."

The will thus pursuant to the maxim of happiness vacillates between motivations, wondering what it should resolve upon. For it considers the outcome, and that is most uncertain: one must have a good head on his shoulders to disentangle himself from the jumble of arguments and counterarguments and not to deceive himself in the tally. But if he asks himself where his duty lies, he is not in the least embarrassed for what answer to give himself; he is instantly certain what he must do. In fact, if the concept of duty carries any weight with him, he will actually shudder to think of benefits he might derive from its violation, just as if he still had a choice.

It is clear, then, that these distinctions are not the niceties they seem to be to Herr G. They are graven into the human soul in the crudest, most legible script, and Herr G.'s argument that *they evaporate altogether when it comes to action* contradicts our experience. Not, of course, the experience embodied in the history of maxims derived from one principle or the other, for this unfortunately shows that most of these maxims flow from the principle of self-interest. But it contradicts the experience, which can only be an inner experience, that no idea does more to lift the human spirit and to fan its enthusiasm than the very idea of a pure moral character. Due to this idea, man will revere his duty above all else, will wrestle with the countless ills of life as well as with its most seductive temptations, and yet (as we correctly assume that he can) will overcome them. That he knows he can do this because he ought to—this is the revelation of divine tendencies within himself deep enough to fill him with sacred awe, as it were, at the magnitude and sublimity of his true destiny. And if it were more frequently brought to the attention of men, if they became accustomed to divesting virtue of the rich loot of advantages to be gained by the performance of duty, and to envisioning virtue in all its purity; if constant use of this view were made a principle of private and public education (a method of inculcating virtue that has been neglected in almost every age)—if these things were done, the state of human morality would improve in short order. The fact that historical experience until now has not yet proved the doctrines of virtue successful may well be due to the wrong premise. The motivating force derived from the idea of duty itself has been considered far too refined for the vulgar understanding; while the cruder idea of duty, based upon certain benefits expected in this world (and indeed in a future world) from following the law (without regard to its motivating force) was credited with a more vigorous effect upon the mind. And it may be due to the adoption of the educational and homiletic principle of preferring the pursuit of happiness over the supreme requirement of reason: being worthy of happiness. The *prescriptions* how to gain happiness, or at least to keep from harm, are not *commandments*. They are not downright obligatory on anyone. Having been warned, man may choose what seems good to him if he is willing to suffer the consequences. Ill effects are apt to result from his failure to take the advice received, but he has no reason to regard them as punishment. Punishment is reserved for a will that is free but unlawful; nature and inclination cannot legislate for freedom. With regard to the idea of duty the situation is entirely different. The violation of one's duty, even without taking into consideration the disadvantages that follow, directly affects the mind of the agent and makes him reprehensible and punishable in his own eyes.

Here we have clear proof that in ethics what is right in theory must work in practice.

As a human being, a creature whose own reason subjects him to certain duties, everybody is a *businessman*. And since, being human, he never outgrows the school of wisdom, he cannot assume that experience has taught him more about what man is or what can be required of him. He cannot send the adherents of theory back to their academies with proud disdain, for none of his experience helps him to escape precepts of theory. It may perhaps help him to learn how theory, once taken into our principles, could be better and more generally put to work; but here we are speaking, not of such pragmatic skills, but of principles.

II. On the Relation of Theory to Practice in Constitutional Law

(*contra* Hobbes)

Among the contracts that enable groups of people to unite in a society (*pactum sociale*), the one to found a civil constitution between them (*pactum unionis civilis*) is a special kind. As far as *execution* is concerned, it has much in common with any other contract aimed at the joint promotion of some purpose; it is essentially different from the rest, however, in the principle of what it founds (*constitutionis civilis*). The union of many people for some common end which they all *have* is found in all social contracts. But their union as an end in itself—as the end that everyone *ought to have*, and thus as the first and unconditioned duty in each external relationship of human beings who cannot avoid influencing one another—does not occur in a society unless it has attained to the civil state, i.e., unless it constitutes a community. The end, now, which in such an external relation is in itself a duty, and itself the supreme formal condition of all other external duties (*conditio sine qua non*), is the legal order (the right) of people *under public coercive laws*, by which each can be assigned his own, and each protected against the incursions of all others.

Yet the concept of external law as such derives completely from the concept of *freedom* in the external relations of men to one another. It has nothing whatever to do with the pursuit of happiness, the end which all men have by nature, or with the prescription of means to that end. There simply must not be any mingling of that law as such with the end of happiness posing as its determining ground. *Law* is the limitation of each man's freedom to the condition of its consistency with everyone's freedom to the extent possible in accordance with a universal law. And *public law* is the totality of the *external laws* that serve to make such thoroughgoing consistency possible. Since every limitation of freedom by another's arbitrary will is termed coercion, it follows that a civil constitution is a relationship of *free* men who are nonetheless subject to coercive laws, their overall freedom in relation to others notwithstanding. They are subject to those laws because reason itself wills it so, pure reason which legislates a priori and irrespective of the empirical ends that have been summed up under the general name happiness. For human ideas regarding those ends differ greatly, and each man seeks them in a different place, so that their will cannot be brought under a common principle nor, consequently, under an external law consistent with everyone's freedom.

The civil state, viewed purely as a legal state, is thus based a priori upon the following principles:

1. The *freedom* of each member of society as a *human being;*
2. The *equality* of each member with every other member as a *subject of the state;*
3. The *independence* of each member of the community as a *citizen.*

These principles are not laws given by a state already established, but they are the only laws that make it possible to found a state in accordance with pure rational principles of external human law as such. Therefore:

1. Human *freedom* as a principle for the constitution of a community I express in this formula: No man can compel me to be happy after his fashion, according to his conception of the wellbeing of someone else. Instead, everybody may pursue his happiness in the manner that seems best to him, provided he does not infringe on other people's freedom to pursue similar ends, i.e., on another's right to do whatever can coexist with every man's freedom under a possible universal law.

If a government were founded on the principle of benevolence toward the people, as a *father's* toward his children—in other words, if it were a *paternalistic government (imperium paternale)* with the subjects, as minors, unable to tell what is truly beneficial or detrimental to them, obliged to wait for the head of state to judge what should constitute their happiness and be kind enough to desire it also—such a government would be the worst conceivable *despotism.* It would be a constitution that cancels every freedom of the subjects, who retain no rights at all. A *patriotic* rather than *paternalistic* government (*imperium, non paternale, sed patrioticum*) is the only one conceivable for people capable of having rights, and also the only one conceivable for a benevolent ruler. For the *patriotic* way of thinking is that which makes everyone in the state, including the ruler, look upon the community as his mother's womb, or on the country as his father's land where he himself came into being, and which he must leave behind as a cherished pledge, in order to protect the rights of the community by laws issuing from the common will, not deeming himself entitled to subject it to the uses of his unconditional discretion.

This right to freedom belongs to every member of the community as a human being, provided he is a being capable of having rights at all.

2. The *equality* of subjects may be phrased as follows: Each member of the community has rights that entitle him to coerce every other member. Only the community's head is excepted from that coercion. Not being a member of the community but its creator or preserver, he alone is authorized to coerce without being subject to legal coercion himself. Whoever is *subject* to laws in a state is a subject; that is to say, coercion by law applies to him as to all other members of the community, with the sole exception of one single (physical or moral) person, the head of state, who is the only one capable of exerting all legal coercion. For if he too could be coerced he would not be the head of the state, and the sequence of subordination would continue upwards ad infinitum. And if there were two persons free from coercion, neither of them would be subject to coercive laws and neither one could wrong the other—which is impossible.

291

But this thorough equality of persons as the subjects of a state is quite consistent with the greatest inequality in the quantity and degree of their possessions, whether these be physical or mental superiority, external gifts of fortune, or simply rights (of which there can be many) with respects to others. One man's welfare, therefore, is greatly dependent on another's will, as the poor man's on the will of the rich; one must obey, as a child its parents or a wife her husband, when the other commands; or, one will serve as a day-laborer while the other pays wages, and so forth. And yet, as subjects all of them are equal *before the law* which, as the expression of the general will, can only be singular, and concerns the form of the right, not the matter or the object to which I have a right. For it is only by means of the public law and its executor, the head of state, that a man can coerce anyone else, but by the same means everyone else will resist him in like measure; and no one can lose this capacity to coerce—i.e., to have rights against others—except in consequence of his own crime. Nor can a man give it up of his own accord; there is no contract, no legal act, by which he can put himself in the position of having no rights any more, only duties. For if he were to do so, he would be depriving himself of the right to make a contract, and so the contract would cancel itself.

This idea of the human equality of men as subjects in a community results in the following formula: Each member of the community must be permitted to rise in it to any status or class (appropriate to a subject) to which his talent, industry, and luck may take him. And his fellow subjects may not block his way by any *hereditary* prerogative, as members of some specific privileged class, to keep him and his heirs beneath that class forever.

For right consists merely in limiting everybody else's freedom to the point where it can coexist with my freedom according to a universal law, and the public law in a community is no more than a state of actual legislation in accordance with this principle and combined with power. Due to his legislation, consequently, all members of a people live as subjects in a state of law (*status iuridicus*), namely, in a state of equilibrium between the effect and counter-effect of wills that limit each other in accordance with the universal law of freedom. This is what we call the civil state; and in that state the *innate right* of everyone is the *same* (i.e., until he takes an action affecting that right), entitling him to compel all others to observe the bounds within which their use of their feedom is compatible with mine. Since a man's birth is not an *action* of his and thus does not bring upon him unequal legal status, nor subject him to any coercive laws other than those which he, as a subject of the sole supreme lawmaking power, shares with all the rest, there can be no one member of the community, no fellow subject, who is innately privileged over another. No man can leave to his descendants any prerogative of the *status* he holds in the community; nor can he forcibly keep them, who are qualified by birth to be masters, so to speak, from rising by their own merits to higher levels in the order of ranks—where one is superior, another inferior, though neither is *imperans* while the other is *subiectus*. A man may leave his heirs everything else; he can bequeath whatever is material and does not concern the person, whatever can be acquired and disposed of as property; and in a sequence of descendants, considerable inequality of financial circumstances may result between the members of a community, between wage earners, tenants, landowners and the laborers who till the land, and so on. Only one thing he cannot prevent: the right of the less favored to rise to the same favored circumstances if enabled to do so by their talent, industry, and luck. For otherwise the testator would be allowed to coerce without being coercible in turn by the reaction of others, and would exceed the level of a fellow subject.

Nor can a man living in the legal framework of a community be stripped of this quality by anything save his own crime. He can never lose it, neither by contract nor by acts of war (*occupatio bellica*), for no legal act, neither his own nor another's, can terminate his proprietary rights in himself. No such act can put him into the class of domestic animals which we use at will for any kind of service and keep in that state without their consent for as long as we please, albeit with the restriction—sometimes religiously sanctioned, as among the Hindus—that they not be mained or killed. No matter what his circumstances, a man may be deemed happy as long as he knows that the law does not discriminate in favor of his fellow subjects, that if he fails to rise to their level it is not due to the irresistible will of others but solely to himself, to his own faculties or resolve, or to circumstances for which he can hold no one else responsible.*

but whole soc/pollec syster [handwritten marginalia]

3. *Independence* (*sibisufficientia*) of a member of a community as a *citizen*, that is to say, a co-legislator. With regard to legislation all men are free and equal *under* public law as already enacted, though they are not equal with respect to the right to *enact* that law. Those who are not able to have this right are still, as members of the community, required to obey its law, and share in its protection, though not as *citizens* but only as *partakers* in the law's protection.

For all rights depend upon laws. But a public law that determines what all men are to be legally permitted or forbidden is the act of a public will from which all rights issue, and which must therefore

---

* If we want to link the word "gracious" with a determinate concept differentiating it from "kind," "benevolent," "protective," and the like, we can use it only for a person who is not subject to legal coercion. In other words, since it is the head of the *state government* who effects and grants every benefit possible under public law (for the *sovereign* who gives those laws is invisible, as it were; he is the law personified, not its agent), that head alone, as the only one not subject to legal coercion, can rightly be titled "gracious lord." Even in an aristocracy, as in Venice for example, the *Senate* is the only "gracious lord." All the nobles who constitute it are subjects (not even the *Doge* excepted, for the Grand Council alone is the sovereign) and, as far as the execution of the laws is concerned, the equals of everyone else. Every subject has the right to coerce any one of them.

Princes—i.e., those who have a hereditary right to the rule—are styled "gracious lords" by courtesy, court fashion, on account of their prospects and claims; but in their proprietary status they are fellow subjects nonetheless, and their humblest servant must have the right to coerce them legally through the head of state.

As for the gracious (more properly, noble) ladies, it might be considered that it is their *status* together with their *sex* which gives them a claim to this title (a claim, consequently, only upon the male sex), and this owing to the refinement of manners (called gallantry), whereby the male believes to do himself greater honor in proportion as he concedes greater prerogatives to the fair sex.

be incapable of wronging anyone. There is but one will for which this is possible: the will of the people as a whole (when all decide about all, and each, accordingly, decides about himself)—because the one man to whom each person can do no legal wrong is himself. If it is otherwise, any decision made for all by a will other than the will of all might be an injustice, and a further law would still be required to limit such a will's enactments. Thus no particular will can serve as lawmaker for a community. (In fact, the very concept of a community is made up of the coinciding concepts of the external freedom, the equality, and the *unity* of the will of *all* and, since the combination of the first two requires voting, independence is the premise of the last.) This basic law, which can emerge only from the general, united popular will, is called the *original contract.*

Every man who has the right to vote on this legislation is termed a *citizen (citoyen,* i.e., a *citizen* of the *state,* not of a city or borough, a *bourgeois).* The only necessary qualification, aside from the *natural* one of not being a child or a woman, is that he be *his own master (sui iuris):* that he own some sort of property—among which may be counted any skill, craft, fine art, or science that supports him. This is to say that whenever he needs to acquire things from others in order to live, he will acquire them only by *disposing* of what is *his own,** not by allowing others to use his services, so that

---

* The producer of an *opus* can convey it to another by transfer, just as if it were his property; but *praestatio operae* is not such a transfer. The domestic servant, the shop clerk, the laborer, even the hairdresser—these are mere *operarii,* not *artifices* in the broader sense, and they are not members of the state, hence not entitled to be citizens. Although my relations to the man I give my firewood to cut, and to the tailor to whom I give my cloth with which to make me a garment, seem altogether similar, yet the first differs from the second as the haidresser differs from the wigmaker (even if I have given him the hair for my wig) or the day-laborer from the artist or craftsman who fashions a work that belongs to him until he has been paid. The latter, acting as a tradesman, will exchange his property (*opus*) with others; the former will permit others to ues his services (*operam*).

It is, I confess, somewhat difficult to determine just what it takes to be able to claim the status of being one's own master.

he will not, in the proper sense of the word, be anyone's servant but the community's. Here, then, craftsmen and large (or small) landowners are all equal, each entitled to cast one vote only. We may disregard the question how one man can have rightly come to own more land than his own hands can put to use (for acquisition by armed conquest is not original acquisition), and how so many who otherwise would have been capable of acquiring permanent property happen to be reduced to serving that landowner for their livelihood. In any event it would conflict with the previous principle, equality, if the large landowning class were so privileged by law that either its descendants would always remain large landowners (of the feudal type, whose estates could not be divided by sale or inheritance so as to benefit more of the people), or that in case of such division none but members of a certain, arbitrarily chosen class could acquire any part of the estates. The large landed proprietor eliminates the votes of as many smaller proprietors as could occupy his place; thus he is not voting in their name and, consequently, has only one vote.

It is necessary, then, to rely exclusively on the ability, industry, and luck of each community member, that these will enable each of them in time to acquire a part of the community, and enable all to acquire the whole. But these differences cannot be taken into account in the making of the general laws. The number of eligible voters on legislation must be set one per capita of property owners, and not according to the size of their possessions.

Yet *all* of those who have this right to vote must agree that the public law is just. Otherwise there would be a legal conflict between those who agree and those who disagree, and the resolution of that conflict would require an additional, higher principle of law. Since we cannot expect unanimity of a whole people, however, the only attainable outcome to be foreseen is a majority of votes—and not a majority of direct voters, in a large nation, but only a majority of those delegated as representatives of the people. The acceptance by general consent, hence by *contract*, of the principle that this majority suffices must be the supreme ground on which to establish a civil constitution.

CONCLUSIONS

Here we have an original contract on which alone a civil and thus consistently legal constitution among men can be based and a community established.

Yet this contract, which we call *contractus originarius* or *pactum sociale,* as the coalition of every particular and private will within a people into a common public will for purposes of purely legal legislation, need by no means to be presupposed as a fact. It is not necessary first to demonstrate historically, so to speak, that a people, whose rights and duties we have inherited, must really have performed such an act *at some time* and must have left us, by word of mouth or in writing, some reliable news or instrument of it, before we are to consider ourselves bound by an existing civil constitution. It is rather a *mere idea* of reason, albeit one with indubitable practical reality, obligating every lawmaker to frame his laws so that they *might* have come from the united will of an entire people, and to regard any subject who would be a citizen as if he had joined in voting for such a will. For this is the touchstone of the legitimacy of all public law. If a law is so framed that all the people *could not possibly* give it their consent—as, for example, a law granting the hereditary *privilege* of *master status* to a certain class of *subjects*—the law is unjust; but if it is *at all possible* that a people might agree on it, then the people's duty is to look upon the law as just, even assuming that their present situation or the tenor of their present way of thinking were such that, if consulted, they would probably refuse to agree.*

---

* If, for example, a proportional war tax were levied on all subjects, the fact that it is onerous would not permit them to call it unjust on the grounds that the war, in their view, was unnecessary. This they have no right to judge, because there is always *the possibility* that the war is unavoidable and the tax indispensable, and hence must be considered lawful in the judgment of the subjects. But if in such a war the property of certain owners is onerously commandeered while others, equally situated, are spared this burden, it is easy to see that all the people cannot consent to such a law, and because they cannot consider such an unequal distribution of burdens as just, they are entitled at least to remonstrate against it.

But this restriction obviously applies to the lawmaker's judgment only, not to the subject's. If a people were to judge that a certain actual legislation will with the utmost probability deprive them of their happiness—what can such a people do? Should they not resist? The answer can be only: they can do nothing but obey. For the question is not what happiness the subject may expect from the establishment of a community or from its administration. Rather, the issue is first of all the legal order which is thereby to be secured for all. This is the supreme principle from which all maxims concerning a community must start, and which is not limited by any other principle. Regarding happiness no universally valid principle of legislation can be given. For both the circumstances of the time and the highly contradictory and constantly changing delusions in which each man seeks his happiness (and no one can prescribe for him where he should seek it) render all fixed principles impossible and unfit by themselves to serve as principles of legislation. The proposition *salus publica suprema civitatis lex est*—the public welfare is the community's highest law—remains undiminished in validity and public esteem; but the common weal to be considered *first of all* is precisely that legal constitution which secures the freedom of everyone by means of laws, leaving him to pursue his happiness by whichever way seems best to him as long as he does not infringe upon that universal freedom under the law and thus upon the rights of other fellow subjects.

When the supreme power makes laws that are initially aimed at happiness—at the prosperity of citizens, at population, and the like —this is not done for the purpose of establishing a civil constitution. It is done simply as a means to *secure the state of law*, chiefly against the people's foreign enemies. The head of state must have the authority to judge by himself alone whether such laws are needed for the community to flourish as it must in order to safeguard its strength and stability, internally as well as against foreign foes. But the purpose is not to make the people happy, against their will as it were; the only purpose is to make them exist as a community.* The lawmaker may err in judging whether or not those measures are *prudently* taken; but there can be no error of judgment when he asks himself whether or not the law is in accord with the legal principle. For here he possesses that infallible yardstick (and a priori at that)—the idea of the original contract. (He need not wait for experience, as he must in following the principle of happiness, to instruct him first about the suitability of his means.) Just as long as it is not self-contradictory to assume that all the people consent to such a law, however distasteful they may find it, the law is in accord with justice. But if a public law is in accord with justice, if it is unimpeachable, irreprehensible from the point of view of the right, it carries with it the authority to coerce and, conversely, a ban on any active resistance to the lawmaker's will. In other words, the power in the state that lends effect to the law is irresistible, and there is no legally existing community that does not have such power to crush all inner resistance, since this resistance would be following a maxim whose general application would destroy all civil constitutions in which alone men can have rights.

It follows that any resistance to the supreme lawmaking power, any incitement of dissatisfied subjects to action, any uprising that bursts into rebellion—that all this is the worst, most punishable crime in a community. For it shatters the community's foundations. And this ban is *absolute,* so unconditional that even though that supreme power or its agent, the head of state, may have broken the original contract, even though in the subject's eyes he may have forfeited the right to legislate by empowering the government to rule tyrannically by sheer violence, even then the subject is allowed no resistance, no violent counteraction. The reason is that once a civil constitution exists, a people no longer have the right to judge

---

* This includes certain import restrictions in order to promote the use of purchasing power for the subjects' own good rather than to benefit foreigners and to stimulate foreign industry; because the state, without a prosperous people, would not be strong enough to resist foreign enemies or to maintain itself as a community.

how that constitution ought to be administered. For suppose they had such a right and their judgment ran counter to that of the actual head of state: who is to decide which side is right? Neither one can act as a judge in his own case. To decide between the head and the people there would have to be a head above the head— which is self-contradictory.

Nor, by the way, can a sort of *right of necessity* (*ius in casu necessitatis*)—which supposed *right* to do *wrong* in extreme (physical) need is an absurdity anyway *—arise here to provide a way in which the barrier blocking the people's own power could be lifted. For the head of state is just as apt to justify his harsh treatment of the subjects by their recalcitrance as they are to justify their rebellion with complaints of their undue suffering at his hands. And who is to decide? The one who is in control of the supreme administration of public justice, and this is precisely the head of state—he alone can decide. And no one in the community can thus have a right to contest that control of his.

And yet there are estimable men who maintain that in certain circumstances the subject does have this right to oppose his superior with force. Among them I will here mention only Achenwall who,

----

* There is only one *casus necessitatis*—the case in which an *absolute duty* conflicts with one that, though perhaps major, is still only a *conditional duty*. For example, to save the state from calamity it may be necessary to betray one's relative, perhaps a father or son. To save the state from calamity is an unconditional duty, but it is only a conditional duty to avert the relative's unhappiness (as long as he has not become guilty of a crime against the state). Reporting a relative's plans to the authorities may be performed with extreme reluctance, but is compelled by necessity, to wit, moral necessity.

But when a shipwrecked man pushes another off his raft to save his own life, then to say that he had a right to do so because of his (physical) need is totally false. For I have a duty to save my life only on condition that I can do so without committing a crime. But I have an unconditional duty not to take the life of someone else who is not injuring me nor even causing the danger threatening mine. Even so, the professors of law are quite consistent in making legal allowance for such emergency acts. For the authorities cannot attach any *punishment* to this injunction, because that punishment would have to be death. And it would be an absurd law that threatened death to one who refuses to die voluntarily in a dangerous situation.

in presenting his doctrines of natural law,* exhibits great caution, precision, and modesty. He says: "If the danger from enduring further the injustice of its head poses a greater threat to the community than may be feared from taking up arms against him, then the people may resist him; on the strength of this right they may set aside their contract of submission and depose him as a tyrant." And he concludes: "In this fashion (respective to their former overlord) the people return to a state of nature."

I can well believe that in an actual case neither Achenwall nor any of the good men who have aired their minds in agreement with him on this point would ever have lent their counsel or consent to such dangerous undertakings. And as for the uprisings in which the Swiss, the Dutch, or even the British won their much vaunted constitutions, there can be hardly a doubt that if those revolts had miscarried, readers of their history would view the execution of their now so exalted initiators as nothing more than the well-earned punishment of high political criminals. For the outcome usually colors our judgment of the legal grounds, though it was uncertain while the latter are certain. As far as these legal grounds are concerned—granting even that such a rebellion might do no wrong to a prince (who may have violated, say, a *joyeuse entrée,* or an actual underlying contract with his people)—it is clear that the people by pursuing their rights in this manner have done the greatest wrong. For this manner, if adopted as a maxim, would render every legal constitution insecure and introduce a state of utter lawlessness (*status naturalis*) in which all rights would lose at least their effectiveness.

Since so many right-thinking authors have this tendency to argue the people's case (to the people's own ruin), I will note only that this is due, at times, to a common fallacy whereby, while talking of the principle of right, they shift the ground of their judgment to the principle of happiness. At other times, no document can be produced of a contract actually submitted to the community, accepted by its head, and sanctioned by both. Having assumed the idea of an original contract—an idea that always provides the

---

* *Ius Naturae. Editio 5ta. Paris posterior, sections 203-206.*

rational basis—to be something that must have happened in *actual fact*, they believe the people to have always retained the right to depart from the contract whenever, in the people's own judgment, there is a gross violation of it.*

It is plain to see here what mischief the principle of happiness (and happiness is really incapable of any determinate principle) causes in constitutional law, just as it does in morality, despite the best intentions of those who teach it. The sovereign wants to make the people happy according to his own notions and becomes a despot; the people will not be deprived of the universal human claim to their own happiness and become rebels. If one had asked, to begin with, what is right—and the principles of this are a priori certain and cannot be bungled by any empiricist—the idea of the social contract would retain its unimpeachable prestige. It would not do so as a fact, as Danton would have it when he declares that without such a fact all property and all rights contained in the actually existing constitution are null and void. But the idea would retain its prestige solely as the rational principle for judging any public lawful constitution as such. And one would see that until a general will exists, the people possess no right at all to coerce their ruler, since it is only through him that they can legally coerce. Yet, once that general will exists, there can be no popular coercion of the ruler, because then the people themselves would be the supreme ruler. Consequently, the people never have any right of coercion (any right to be refractory in word or deed) against the head of state.

This theory is also amply confirmed in practice. In Great Britain,

---

* No matter how the people's real contract with their sovereign may be violated, they cannot immediately react *as a community,* but only as a mob. For the former constitution has been torn up by the people, while their organization as a new *community* is still to occur. This is when the state of anarchy arises with all its at least potential horrors. And the wrong in that situation is whatever each of the people's parties inflicts on the other. This also emerges from an example cited, where the rebellious subjects of that state finally sought to force on each other a constitution that would have become far more oppressive than the one discarded—namely, the prospect of being devoured by clerics and aristocrats instead of being able to look to an all-governing head for a more equitable distribution of the state's burdens.

whose people boast of their constitution as if it were the model for all the world, we nonetheless find the constitution completely silent on what the people have a right to do in case the monarch should transgress the contract of 1688. In other words: if he wanted to violate it, the constitution, in the absence of any specific law, secretly reserves the right to rebel. That the constitution should contain a law for such a case—a law to justify the overthrow of the existing constitution which is the source of all particular laws (even assuming a breach of contract)—is a clear contradiction, because then it would have to contain a publicly constituted * opposing power, a second head of state to protect the people's right against the first. And there would have to be a third, then, to decide which of the two sides is right.

Worried, moreover, about such charges in the event their enterprise should fail, those popular guides (or guardians, if you will) who frightened the monarch away preferred to impute to him a voluntary surrender of the reins of government rather than to arrogate to themselves a right to depose him—a claim that would have brought the constitution into a flagrant contradiction with itself.

Surely I will not be accused of flattering the monarch too much with this kind of inviolability; and so I hope also to be spared the charge of favoring the people too much when I say that they, too, have inalienable rights against the head of state, even though these rights cannot be coercive.

Hobbes is of the opposite opinion. According to him (*de Cive*, chapter 7, section 14) the head of state is bound by no contractual obligation toward the people. He cannot wrong the citizens, he may dispose of them as he wishes. This thesis would be quite true if "wrong" were understood to give the injured a coercive right against the man who inflicted the wrong; but stated in such general terms the proposition is terrifying.

---

* No right in the state can be insidiously concealed, as it were, by way of a secret reservation, least of all the right which the people presume to be a part of the constitution. For all constitutional laws must be conceived as deriving from a public will. If the constitution were to permit rebellion, it would have to state publicly the right to rebel and the way to exercise it.

The nonrecalcitrant subject must be able to assume that his sovereign does not *want* to wrong him. On this assumption, since every man has inalienable rights which he cannot give up even if he would, and concerning which he is himself entitled to judge, the wrong that a citizen believes himself to have suffered can be due only to an error, or to the ignorance of certain consequences that follow from laws made by the supreme power. Accordingly the citizen must be free to inform the public of his views on whatever in the sovereign decrees appears to him as a wrong against the community, and he must have this freedom with the sovereign's own approval. For to assume that the head might never be in error, never in ignorance of anything, would be to imagine him graced with divine intuitions and exalted above all men. *Freedom of the pen*—within the bounds of respect and affection for the constitution one lives under, kept within those bounds by the subjects' liberal way of thinking which the constitution itself instills in them (and to which the pens automatically restrict one another, lest they lose their freedom)—this is the sole shield of popular rights. For to deny the people this freedom would not merely deprive them of every claim to justice in regard to the supreme commander according to Hobbes); it would also deprive the supreme commander, whose will commands the subjects as citizens only by representing the general will of the people, of any knowledge of matters which he himself would change if only he knew them. Hence, to limit this freedom would bring him into contradiction with himself. But to make the head apprehensive that public unrest might be incited if men were to think for themselves and to think out loud amounts to arousing in him distrust of his own power or even hatred of his own people.

There is a universal principle by which a people must judge its rights *negatively*—i.e., must judge what the supreme legislature, in all good faith, might be deemed *not to have ordained*. This principle is contained in the proposition: *Whatever resolution the people cannot make about themselves, the lawmaker cannot make about the people.*

Suppose, for example, a law were to command the permanent establishment of a previously decreed state religion. Could this be viewed as expressing the lawmaker's real will and intent? One should first ask himself whether a people *may* enact a law to the effect that certain tenets of faith and outward religious forms, once adopted, should remain forever; that is, may a people prevent itself (in its future generations) from progressing in religious insight or from correcting what may be old errors? It will be clear then that an original contract in which the people made such a law would be null and void in itself, because it runs counter to the destiny and to the ends of mankind. A law so made is thus not to be regarded as the monarch's true will, and remonstrances may be made to him.

But in each case in which something of the kind has nevertheless been decreed by supreme legislation, general and public judgments on it may be offered, but resistance in word or deed must never be mobilized.

What must prevail in every community is *obedience,* bowing to coercive laws that suffer no exception within the mechanism of the state constitution. But at the same time a *spirit of freedom* must prevail, since in matters of universal human duty everyone wants to be rationally convinced of the justice of this coercion, lest he come into contradiction with himself. Obedience without the spirit of freedom is the effective cause of all *secret societies.* For it is a natural calling of mankind to communicate with one another, especially about what concerns man in general; with the cultivation of this feedom those societies would disappear.

And how else could a government obtain the knowledge that promotes its own essential intent than by allowing the spirit of freedom, a spirit so worthy of respect both in its origin and its effects, to express itself?

✽   ✽   ✽

Nowhere will a practice that avoids all pure rational principles disparage theory more arrogantly than in the question of what a good state constitution requires. This is because a long-standing legal constitution gradually causes the people to make it their rule to judge both their happiness and their rights by the state of affairs in which everything so far has functioned peacefully—but not, conversely, to evaluate the state of affairs by concepts of both their rights and happiness with which reason supplies them. The rule is, rather, always to prefer that passive state to the perilous position of seeking a better one, a position to which Hippocrates' advice to physicians applies: *iudicium anceps, experimentum periculosum*— decision is difficult, experiment perilous. All constitutions of sufficiently long standing, whatever their flaws and for all their differences, yield the same result: one is content with the constitution one lives under. Hence, from the viewpoint of *the people's welfare,* no theory properly applies at all; instead, everything rests on a practice submissive to experience.

But if there is something in reason which the term "constitutional law" can express, and if men who face each other in the antagonism of their freedom find in this concept a unifying force—if it shows them an objective, practical reality (and here no reference must be made to whatever well-being or ill-being it may cause them, for that can be learned only by experience)—it is based on a priori principles, because experience cannot teach us what is right. And then, there is a *theory* of constitutional law with which all practice, to be valid, must agree.

The only argument to be advanced against this thesis is that while men have in their heads the idea of rights that are their due, their hard hearts make them incapable and unworthy of being treated accordingly, so that they may and must be kept in order by a supreme power acting solely on rules of prudence. Yet this desperate leap (*salto mortale*) is such that, once we are talking not of right but of power only, the people may try their own power and jeopardize every legal constitution. Unless there is something which rationally compels immediate respect, such as human rights, all influences upon human choice will be incapable of curbing human freedom. But when the right, joined by benevolence, makes its voice heard, human nature shows itself not too depraved to listen deferentially. (*Tum pietate gravem meritisque si forte virum quem/ Conspexere silent arrectisque auribus adstant:* Once they behold a man weighty with merits and righteousness, they stand in silence, pricking up their ears. Virgil.)

III. On the Relation of Theory to Practice in International Law—A General-Philanthropic, i.e., Cosmopolitan View *

(*contra* Mendelssohn)

Are we to love the human race as a whole, or is it an object to be viewed with displeasure, an object that has our best wishes (lest we become misanthropic) but never our best expectations, and from which, therefore, we would rather avert our eyes?

The answer to this question depends on our answer to another question. Are there tendencies in human nature which allow us to infer that the species will always progress toward the better, and that the evil of present and past times will be lost in the good of the future? If so, we could love the species at least for its constant approach to the good; if not, we would have to loathe or despise it, no matter what the affectations of a universal love of mankind—which would then be, at most, a well-meaning love, not a love well pleased—may say to the contrary. What is and remains evil, notably the evil and deliberate mutual violation of the most sacred human rights, this we cannot avoid loathing, even when we try our hardest to love it. We hate it—not that we would harm people, but that we would have as little to do with them as possible.

---

* It is not immediately apparent how a general-*philanthropic* presupposition relates to a *cosmopolitan* constitution, and how the latter relates to the foundation of international law as the only condition in which those human tendencies that make our species lovable can be properly developed. The conclusion of this part will make that connection plain.

Moses Mendelssohn was of the latter opinion (*Jerusalem*, Section Two, pp. 44-47), opposing it to his friend Lessing's hypothesis of mankind undergoing a divine education. To him it is chimera "that the whole of mankind down here should be moving ever forward, perfecting itself in the sequence of times."

We see, he says, the human race as a whole "performing slight oscillations, and it has never taken a few forward steps without relapsing soon after, twice as fast, into its former condition." (This is exactly the boulder of Sisyphus; in this way one assumes, with the Hindus, that the earth is a place of penance for old sins now beyond recall.) "Men progress but mankind constantly wavers within the same fixed limits; viewed as a whole it maintains at all periods of time about the same level of morality, the same measure of religion and irreligion, virtue and vice, happiness(?) and misery."

He introduces this assertion (p. 46) by saying, "You want to guess what Providence intends for mankind? Forge no hypotheses" (earlier he had called them "theory"); "just look around at what is really happening, and if you can, survey the history of all ages and look at what has happened from the beginning. This is the fact; this must have been part of the intention; this must have been approved or at least included in the plans of wisdom."

I take a different view.

If it is a sight fit for a god to see a virtuous man wrestle with tribulations and temptations and yet stand firm, it is a sight most unfit, I will not say for a god, but for the commonest man of good will to see the human race from period to period take upward steps toward virtue, only to see it soon after relapsing just as deeply into vice and misery. To watch this tragedy for a while may perhaps be touching and instructive, but eventually the curtain has to fall. For in the long run the tragedy becomes a farce, and though the actors, fools that they are, do not tire of it, the spectator will. After one or two acts he has had enough of it; he can correctly assume that the never-ending play is forever the same. If it is only a play, the punishment at the end may make up for his unpleasant sensations. But in real life to pile vice upon countless vice (though interrupted by virtues), just so that some day there will be plenty to punish, would be repugnant, at least by our conception, even to the morality of a wise creator and governor of the world.

I may be allowed to assume, therefore, that our species, progressing steadily in civilization as is its natural end, is also making strides for the better in regard to the moral end of its existence, and that this progress will be *interrupted* now and then, but never *broken off*. I do not have to prove this assumption; the burden of proof is on its opponent. I rest my case on this: I have the innate duty (though in respect of moral character required I am not so good as I should and hence could be) so to affect posterity through each member in the sequence of generations in which I live, simply as a human being, that future generations will become continually better (which also must be assumed to be possible), and that this duty may thus rightfully be passed on from one generation to the next. Let any number of doubts be drawn from history to dispute my hopes, doubts which, if conclusive, might move me to abandon a seemingly futile labor; but as long as the futility cannot be made wholly certain, I cannot exchange my duty (as the *liquidum*) for the rule of prudence not to attempt the unfeasible (as the *illiquidum*, because it is a mere hypothesis). I may always be and remain unsure whether an improvement in the human race can be hoped for; but this can invalidate neither the maxim nor its necessary presupposition that in a practical respect it be feasible.

Without this hope for better times the human heart would never have been warmed by a serious desire to do something useful for the common good; this hope has always influenced the labors of right-thinking men. Even the excellent Mendelssohn must have reckoned with it when he so zealously strove for the enlightenment and welfare of the nation to which he belonged. For he could not reasonably hope to accomplish them by himself, all alone, unless others after him continued advancing on the same path. Despite the depressing sight, not so much of ills that oppress mankind from natural causes as of those men inflict upon each other, the mind is cheered by the prospect that things may be better in future—a quite unselfish benevolence, since we shall long be in our graves and shall not reap the fruits which we have helped to sow. Empirical arguments against the success of these resolves, which rest on hope, are insufficient here. The argument that what has not succeeded so far will therefore never succeed, does not even justify the abandonment of a pragmatic or technological intention (as that of air travel by aerostatic balloons, for instance), much less than abandonment of a moral intention that becomes a duty unless its accomplishment is demonstrably impossible. Besides, there is a good deal of evidence to show that in our age, compared with all earlier ones, mankind has by and large really made considerable moral progress for the better. (Short-time arrests can prove nothing to the contrary.) And it can also be shown that the screaming about an irresistibly growing depravation of mankind comes from the very fact that, upon reaching a higher level of morality, we can see farther ahead, and that the severity of our judgments about what we are compared with what we ought to be—in other words, our self-criticism— increases the higher we have climbed on the moral ladder in all of what we have come to know of the world's course.

If we ask, then, by what means we might maintain and possibly accelerate this perpetual progress for the better, we soon see that this immeasurable success will depend not so much on what *we* do (on what education we give to the young, for instance), or on the method *we* ought to use to accomplish it. Instead, it will depend upon what human *nature* will do in and with us to *force* us onto a track to which we would not easily accommodate ourselves on our own. For we can look only to nature, or rather, because the attainment of this end requires supreme wisdom, the *Providence* for a success that will affect the whole and thence the parts, while on the contrary, the *designs* of men start with the parts, if indeed they do not stop there. The whole as such is too large for men; they can extend their ideas to it, but not their influence, chiefly since the design of one man will repel another, so that they would hardly reach agreement on a design of their own free intention.

Just as universal violence and the resulting distress were finally bound to make a people decide that they would submit to the coercion of public laws, which reason itself prescribes for them as remedy, and found a state under a *civil constitution,* even so the distress of ceaseless warfare, in which states in turn seek to reduce or subjugate each other, must eventually bring the states under a *cosmopolitan* constitution even against their will. Such general peace may pose an even greater threat to freedom from another quarter by leading to the most terrible despotism, as has repeatedly happened in the case of oversized states. Yet the distress of ceaseless warfare must compel them to adopt a condition which, although not a cosmopolitan community under one head, is still lawful—a *federation* under jointly agreed *international law*.

For the advancing civilization of the states, accompanied by a growing inclination to expand by cunning or by force at the other's expense, means the multiplication of wars. To maintain standing armies, to add to them constantly more men at the same pay, to keep them in training and equip them with ever more numerous tools of war, all this is bound to produce higher and higher costs. The price of all necessities keeps rising, without any hope of a corresponding increase in the supply of the metals of which they are made. And no peace lasts long enough for the peacetime savings to match the cost of the next war, a complaint for which the invention of national debts is an ingenious but ultimately self-destructive nostrum. As a result, impotence must finally accomplish what good will ought to have done but did not: the organization of every state's internal affairs so that the decisive voice on whether or not to wage war is not that of the head of state—whom the war costs actually nothing—but that of the people, who pay for it. (This necessarily presupposes, of course, the realization of that idea of the original contract.) For the people are hardly likely to plunge themselves into penury—which never touches the head of state—out of sheer lust of expansion or because of supposed purely verbal insults. And so their descendants will not be burdened with debts they have not brought on themselves; they too—due not to any love for them, but only to the self-love of each era—will be able to progress toward an ever better condition, even in a moral sense; because any community unable to harm others by force must rely on justice alone, and may have grounds to hope for help from other communities of the same constitution.

This, however, is just an opinion and mere hypothesis, as uncertain as all judgments claiming to state the sole adequate natural cause for an intended effect that is not wholly in our power. And, as has been shown above, even as such an hypothesis it contains no principle for its enforcement by the subjects of an existing state; rather, it contains an enforcement principle for uncoercible heads of state. In the usual order of things it is not in human nature to relinquish power voluntarily; yet, in pressing circumstances, it is not impossible. So we may consider it a not inadequate expression of the moral hopes and wishes of men (conscious of their weakness) to look to *Providence* for the circumstances required. They may hope that since it is the *purpose* of *mankind*, of the entire species, to achieve its final destiny by the free use of its powers as far as they go, Providence will bring about an outcome to which the purposes of *men*, considered separately, run directly counter. For this very counteraction of inclinations, the fonts of evil, gives reason free play to subjugate them all and to inaugurate a reign of the good that is self-sustaining, once it exists, in place of the reign of self-destructive evil.

*   *   *

Nowhere does human nature appear less lovable than in the relations of whole nations to each other. No state's independence or possessions are even for a moment safe from the others. The will to subjugate another, or encroach upon what belongs to him, is always present; and warlike preparations for defense, which often make peace more burdensome and more destructive of domestic welfare than war itself, may never be relaxed. For this the only possible remedy is international law based on public statutes backed by power, statutes to which every state would have to submit in analogy to civil or constitutional law for individuals. For an enduring universal peace by means of the so-called *balance of power in Europe* is a mere chimera, rather like Swift's house whose architect had built it in such perfect accordance with all the laws of equilibrium that a sparrow lighting on the roof made it promptly collapse.

"But states," it will be said, "will never submit to such coercive laws; and the proposal of a universal international state, whose authority all individual states should voluntarily accept and whose laws they should obey, may sound ever so nice in the theory of an Abbé de Saint-Pierre or a Rousseau, but it will not work in practice. Has it not always been ridiculed by great statesmen, and more yet by heads of state, as a pedantically childish academic idea?"

I for my part put my trust in the theory that proceeds from the principle of justice, concerning how relations between individuals and states *ought to be*. The theory commends to the earthly demigods the maxim to proceed so that each of their quarrels become the introduction to such a universal international state and, thus, to assume as a practical possibility that it *can be*.

At the same time, however, I trust (*in subsidium*) in the nature of things, which compels one to go where he would rather not (*fata volentem ducunt, nolentem trahunt*—fate guides the willing and drags the unwilling). In this I also take human nature into account. Since respect for right and duty is still alive in human nature, I cannot, or will not, consider it so steeped in evil that in the end, after many unsuccessful attempts, moral-practical reason should not triumph and show human nature also to be lovable. So, even from a cosmopolitan viewpoint my assertion stands: what is valid in theory, on rational grounds, is valid also in practice.

KÖNIGSBERG.   I. KANT